THE MAGIC
OF
MANIFESTING MONEY

20 Advanced Manifestation Techniques to Attract Wealth, Success, and Abundance Without Hard Work, Manifesting, The Power of the Mind

MARIA SUNNI

© Copyright 2020 by Maria Sunni All right reserved.

The work contained herein has been produced with the intent to provide relevant knowledge and information on the topic on the topic described in the title for entertainment purposes only. While the author has gone to every extent to furnish up to date and true information, no claims can be made as to its accuracy or validity as the author has made no claims to be an expert on this topic. Notwithstanding, the reader is asked to do their own research and consult any subject matter experts they deem necessary to ensure the quality and accuracy of the material presented herein.

This statement is legally binding as deemed by the Committee of Publishers Association and the American Bar Association for the territory of the United States. Other jurisdictions may apply their own legal statutes. Any reproduction, transmission or copying of this material contained in this work without the express written consent of the copyright holder shall be deemed as a copyright violation as per the current legislation in force on the date of publishing and subsequent time thereafter. All additional works derived from this material may be claimed by the holder of this copyright.

The data, depictions, events, descriptions and all other information forthwith are considered to be true, fair and accurate unless the work is expressly described as a work of fiction. Regardless of the nature of this work, the Publisher is exempt from any responsibility of actions taken by the reader in conjunction with this work. The Publisher acknowledges that the reader acts of their own accord and releases the author and Publisher of any responsibility for the observance of tips, advice, counsel, strategies and techniques that may be offered in this volume.

TABLE OF CONTENTS

Introduction 1

Chapter 1: The Science Behind Attracting Money ... 6

    All Things Are Made Up Of Waves And Particles 7

    Most Of Quantum Physics Is Very Small 11

    The Connection Between Manifestation And Quantum Physics 13

    Everything Is Energy 16

Chapter 2: The Most Common Money Blocks 31

Chapter 3: The Subconscious Mind 53

    The Power Of The Mind 59

    Overcoming The Subconscious Blocks 63

    Creating A Positive Mindset 66

    Taking Down Those Neural Pathways 73

Chapter 4: Creating A Money Mindset 85

    Why Is Mindset Important 91

    Seven Ways To Create A Positive Mindset 99

    Like Attracts Like And Toxic Positivity 106

Chapter 5: Learning What You Want 117

   Coming Up With An Action Plan 119

Chapter 6: Cultivating Gratitude 131

   Fuel For Gratitude 132
   Find Gratitude When Life Is Rough 133
   Growing Your Gratitude 141

Chapter 7: Believing You Can.................................147

   To Radiate Love 148
   Releasing Your Fears 152
   Replacing Your Fears 155
   Doubting The Law Of Attraction 159

Chapter 8: Visualization..162

   The Power Of Visualization 164
   Techniques For Visualization 166
   Creative Visualization 171

Chapter 9: Trusting The Path.................................178

   Faith 178
   Determination 181
   Success Stories 185

Chapter 10: What To Do Once Your Money Reaches You 191

   How To Find Happiness 195

Chapter 11: Honoring Your Value 202

   Is There A Difference Between Self-Value And Self-Worth? 203

   Psychology Behind Self-Worth 206

   What Can Help Determine Self-Worth? 208

Conclusion 227

INTRODUCTION

Congratulations on purchasing this book, and thank you for doing so.

The following chapters will discuss the many aspects of manifesting money into your life and how you can control the process.

Money problems are one of the most common reasons for stress. Most people believe that they are at the mercy of money, so to speak and that they have no real control over it because it always seems to disappear as quickly as they get it. It can be stressful not knowing if you have enough to pay your bills, buy groceries, and get the things you need to survive. What if I told you there was a way where you could stop this cycle of stress simply by changing the way you think?

I'm certain that sounds too good to be true, but it's not. It's actually a very real thing that a lot of people have learned how to harness. I'll be honest, it's not necessarily easy to do, and it probably won't happen as quickly as you would like it to, as most things in life. But you can change your money woes for the better with some simple action steps, and that's what this book is going to cover.

The first thing we will look at, though, is the science behind attracting money. This will show you that it's not just some snake oil, but a real thing that can really work if you learn how to use it properly.

After that, we'll look at blocks that a lot of people have. These are thought processes or beliefs about money that prevent you from attracting money into your life. A lot of people have these blocks because society has drilled them into our heads. That will bring us to the next point of the subconscious mind. This is where most of the manifestation work takes place and is the powerhouse for creating the life you want.

Next, we will start discussing ways to change your mindset so that you attract money instead of pushing it away. This will involve figuring out exactly what it is that you want. That's the important thing here. If you can't say specifically what it is you want, then how can you attract it into your life.

Then we will talk about the importance of gratitude. Gratitude helps in a multitude of ways in your life, so it's really high time that everybody starts learning how to be grateful for the things they have.

After that, we'll talk about the importance of believing that you can attract the things you want. Belief is just as important as gratitude, maybe more so. If you don't believe it, then it's not going to happen. To help you believe, we will talk about visualization. This will help you really get into what you want to attract into your life and experience it as if it were already there.

Along the same lines, we will also talk about trusting the path. As I mentioned already, very rarely do you manifest things into your life when you want them. They happen when they are supposed to, and you have no real control over that. That's why you have to trust you are exactly where you need to be right now, believe that your money is coming to you, and follow your path.

Next, we'll discuss how to act once you have money. You must respect the money you get and handle it appropriately. This part isn't that hard to do. The main thing is to make sure you stay connected with your original goal and appreciate what you have, even if it is a lot more than you had before.

Lastly, we'll talk about the importance of honoring yourself. You have to honor your own worth in order to attract things into your life. If you can't love yourself, then the Universe won't be able to help you out.

There are plenty of books on this subject on the market; thanks again for choosing this one! Every effort was made to ensure it is full of as much useful information as possible. Please enjoy!

CHAPTER 1

THE SCIENCE BEHIND ATTRACTING MONEY

The science behind attracting money is basically quantum physics. Quantum physics is the basic theory of how particles and force work. This creates the foundation of particle physics's standard model, which is one of the most exhaustively tested approaches ever. But it also leaves many people arguing about its efficacy. In order for it to work, you have to assume a lot of basics and counter-intuitive things about how nature works on tiny scales.

For most of us, quantum physics is very intimidating. When it seems weird and counter-intuitive to the physicists who face it daily, why would we see it as anything different? But it really isn't all that incomprehensible. When it comes to reading about quantum physics, there are some concepts that you need to try and remember. If you can master these, then you will find it a lot easier to understand.

All Things Are Made Up of Waves and Particles

There are many different ways to begin talking about this, which is the best place to start. All things within the universe have the nature of particles and waves. While this likely seems crazy, it is an experimental fact that has been worked out through common processes.

Of course, saying that actual objects are both waves and particles is a bit imprecise. The objects that are described by quantum physics aren't particles nor waves, but fall into a third category of shared properties of waves and shared properties of particles. This often causes some debate in the physics community about whether or not to talk about light as a particle during an introduction to physics class. Not because it is controversial, but because referring to photons as "particles" instead of "excitations of a quantum field" could cause some misconceptions.

This third option of quantum objects' nature is that it is often seen as having a confusing language that physicists use to discuss quantum phenomena. The Large Hadron Collider helped to discover the Higgs boson as a particle, but it is also common to hear physicists mention that the "Higgs field" as something delocalized that fills space. This is due to the fact that with some circumstances, like the experiments with the collider, it is easier to talk about the excitations within the Higgs field to emphasize the particle-like aspects. At other times, it is best to talk about physics in terms of how it interacts with the quantum field. It is merely a different language that describes the same object.

It Is Discrete

This can be seen in its name. Quantum originates from a Latin word that means "how much" and shows us that quantum models will always have discrete amounts. The energy of this quantum field is relayed using integer multiples. When it comes to light, this is connected to the wavelength and frequency of the light. Short-wavelength and high-frequency light will always have large characteristic energy, whereas the long-wavelength and low-frequency light will always have low energy.

For both of these, though, the complete amount of energy within a particular light field will always be an integer multiple, like 1, 2, 14, 137 times, and is never a weight fraction such as the square root of two or 1 ½. You can see this property in the atom's discrete energy level, as well as the solid's energy bands. Some energy values can be used while others can't.

It Is Probabilistic

This tends to be the most surprising and one of the most controversial parts of quantum physics in the past. Quantum physics makes it impossible to have complete certainty about what an experiment's outcome may be. If a physicist predicts the outcome, the prediction will always take on the form of figuring out the odds of each possible outcome, and the comparisons between the experiment and theory are always involved in inferring probability distributions from repeat experiments.

The quantum system's math typically comes out as a "wavefunction," which is typically shown within equations using psi. There is quite a bit of debate about what this actually shows. There are two sides to this. One says "wavefunction" is something physical. Two are the ones who believe the "wavefunction" is simply an expression of what we know regarding the state of the quantum object.

Either way, the odds of finding an outcome isn't directly given by the "wavefunction," but instead, by its square. This is what is called the "Born Rule," named after the German physicist Mac Born who came up with the idea.

Most of Quantum Physics is Very Small

A lot of people view quantum physics as something that is weird because it is something different that you often experience day-to-day. This is due to the fact that the effects involved get smaller as objects grow larger. This is why everything in quantum phenomena is tested within particles and atoms because they are small enough to allow physicists to see their wavelengths.

It Is Not Magic

While quantum physics may seem weird, I can assure you that it isn't magic. It predicts strange things due to our everyday physics, but they can all be explained through mathematical principles and rules. That means if somebody tells you about a "quantum" idea that seems way too good to be true, it most likely is. But that doesn't mean we aren't able to use quantum physics to do cool things. The thing is, all of that stays within the confines of the laws of thermodynamics.

That is the core of quantum physics. It is by no means a complete lesson or explanations on the subject, but it will give you a good understanding of the basics. That said, I feel I owe you an explanation as to why, in a manifestation book, I am talking about such a confusing subject as quantum physics.

The Connection Between Manifestation and Quantum Physics

Manifesting the things we want works because of the vibrations and alignment of energies. Quantum physics studies the tiniest particles of energy. Research in quantum physics has found that the simple act of observing reality will create it. Attempting to observe something will make it appear out of nowhere. Plus, if you are not aware of something, then that something does not exist within your reality.

Matter and light are non-existent until something takes place that causes them to become real, but what is that something? Science has called this something the "collapse of the wave function." Further investigation discovered this to be consciousness, which performs the action to create the reality. The wave function holds every possible outcome for a certain situation, but only one of them shows up in the real world once it collapses by a consciousness. How come we see the person instead of the cluster of energy?

Look at it as a movie reel. All a movie is is a collection of around 24 frames a second. Every frame has a small gap the separates it. However, since the speed at which a frame replaces the next, the eyes are cheated into believing we are seeing one continuous, moving picture.

We have five main physical senses: taste, sight, smell, sound, and touch. Every sense has a specific spectrum. For example, a dog is able to hear on a different range that a human can. Basically, your sense perceives energy from a limited standpoint and creates an image based upon that.

Human thoughts are connected to this invisible energy and are able to determine what it creates. Your thoughts will shift the universe through a particle-by-particle basis to make your life. You are able to change your life and environment through observations and views. Your reality is how you perceive it, and if you don't know about something, it doesn't exist. If you want it to be in your life, then perceive it.

There is also a quantum concept known as quantum entanglement that describes the relationship between two things that entangle or interact with one another. After they do, it is impossible to describe one object without thinking about the other. They are now both bonded together.

This connects to manifestation because everything within the universe is connected, and if you can influence one thing, you can influence another. What we are able to influence fully are our thoughts. If you can remember this, you will be able to understand how manifesting actually works.

Everything Is Energy

Because everything is energy, this means that everything is connected to all things in the universe. The clouds, the water that fills the oceans, the animals, trees, me, you, and everything comes from one source, and everything will return to that source. Feelings and thoughts are energy, too. Whatever you feel and think will have an influence on everyone and everything that lives on this planet. If this is true, then we actually have the ability to create our realities since our minds rule over matter.

Quantum physics has offered evidence about this basic fact. It is a huge concept, with the implications being extremely massive. It will give you a migraine if you try to understand all of it. It isn't anything that most people even think about. It does explain our basic existence if you can mix the spiritual aspect with it.

This information is helpful since it is the foundation for figuring out ourselves and the world. This can open us up to life's bigger picture. The hard part is finding a way to explain all of this without completely blowing your mind while making this knowledge useful to be able to get some benefits out of it.

When trying to understand all of this, you are going to encounter a lot of words like resonate and vibrations. This is just an easier way to explain everything. It tells us the ways our senses interpret all that is around us and translates it through vibrations. Quantum physics explains this as "an invisible moving force that can influence our physical realm."

It tells us how we live with the illusion that we limit our world because we think all there is in the world is what our senses are able to interpret. Once you can understand that everything is energy, you have to learn how to relate that to your personal growth and manifestations.

Our five senses can't completely perceive the fact that everything is energy. Once you fully comprehend that everything is energy, you will be able to realize that we just recognize an illusion.

 Although our senses are telling us this can't be true, it is. There is only energy; some people refer to is as source energy, but it is there, and it has various changing forms and frequencies. The main difference is the way energies interact with one another.

Energy will interact with everything at all times, and you won't ever see it. You might be able to sense this energy. Everyone is familiar with talking about our emotions or physical energy as being "energy in motion."

Humans have a wonderful gift of being able to control our thoughts. Everyone has free will and is able to choose where and how to direct our energy. This is a very small percentage if you compare it to the amount of energy we use on our unconscious thoughts.

Our thoughts make an extremely specific vibration, and then this energy will try to find a match to that vibration. You won't even be aware you are doing it. This is similar to pinging a tuning fork. It can cause an object that has the same frequency if it is near enough to vibrate, and they will be in vibrational harmony.

Every single object in the world has its own unique vibration, and all the energy in the world vibrates. A basic law of attraction states energy will attract itself to other energy that it resonates with.

Both the physical and nonphysical features of the universe are nothing but intelligence and energy that vibrates. Nothing ever rests. The main difference between the things we can perceive, whether it can or can't be seen, is how fast it vibrates.

Have you noticed how things seem to happen in waves? You are stuck at home thinking about something when a wave of emotion overtakes your mind and body. When you open your oven door, a wave of heat hits you in the face. If you listen to a thunderstorm, you can hear a wave of thunder. If you are outside on a windy day, you can feel the wave of air as the wind blows your hair. You are outside working in the garden, and you can feel the waves of the sun as it beams down on your skin. You are walking along the shore when waves of the ocean roll over your feet. All kinds of energy will travel in waves. This energy can't ever be destroyed or created; it only changes forms.

Thoughts are also energy. The brain is the most powerful electromagnetic tool that was ever created. Don't worry; you don't have to be a physicist to understand this, but when you begin to understand the concept of everything is energy, you will realize you are able to break this down to usable levels in your own life.

Since humans have free will and consciousness, there are a lot more layers involved since we can create our own beliefs based on the things that we were taught growing up and what we have experienced in life.

This is our personal power, but it can be a challenge since he has a limiting belief system that obstructs the flow of energy inside us that we aren't even aware of most of the time. Our belief systems are also energy, and this is what gets in our way when we try to attract things to us.

Our belief systems are limited to the energy we put behind it, which means it can't be changed. When you finally realize that your belief system isn't working, for example: "I won't ever find a job." Or "I won't ever be able to get out of debt." You could use therapy such as EFT to get rid of certain problems so you can be open to new realities and possibilities.

You are probably going to find some areas of resistance, but you don't have to give it a label of wrong or right. It only showed up because of your point of view or beliefs at that moment in time. Think of it as a gift if you do find them. Notice it, and be grateful you had an opportunity to change it into something that you actually liked.

Everyone is vibrating some kind of energy, and we will attract that same into our lives. We might think that we are focusing on the things we want, but beneath it all, we are actually vibrating, believing, and focusing on the things we don't have. If you can get rid of your low vibrations and subconscious blocks, it will allow you to choose new actions and expand the mind that will then create brand now results.

Focus on your life and see everything you have: your health, your house, your bank account, your job, your partner, and your children. These are all things that you created in your life. Now go back and try to remember the major beliefs and thoughts and see if these match up. If you are completely honest, you should see a correlation between how you thought your life would be and what you thought was possible or what you thought you deserved and were capable of achieving; you might see that your life reflects these limits.

Now that you understand everything is energy and realize that you are nothing but energy, you might feel empowered about your future transformation. If you still don't completely understand, give it some time.

But is everything really energy? Is everything in the world connected? If you were to look around your surroundings right now, you might see your television, laptop, window, and pet; outside, you might see some trees, grass, flowers, or car. Yes, all of these are individual things. Since everything contains the same matter, does this make everything one? The truth is what I see is many phenomena instead of a unified whole. You might have learned that all matter is made from molecules during your school years. You probably learned that all molecules are made up of atoms and contain a nucleus with electrons orbiting around it. All of these are particles, fractions, and parts. But when you first see it, there isn't unity, a whole. It doesn't matter because appearances can be deceiving. What might look like a solid may not be as solid as it looks.

Scientists have proven that matter has 99.999999999999 percent empty space. Yes, there are 12 nines after the decimal. If you were to make the nucleus of an atom as large as a pinhead, the first electron would be 160 feet away. You will find nothing but empty space in between. This means that what you are reading right now, whatever you are sitting on, your house, the Earth, all this "solid reality" is mostly empty spaces. That's a lot of empty spaces. So, what exactly is left when talking about the solid matter? A calculation will show you that the solid part of any atom is just 0.000000000001 percent of the entire atom. It is hard to believe that all solid objects would consist of this little bit of solid matter. If you look at it that way, anything solid really isn't solid.

No Solid Parts

After scientists discovered atoms and molecules during the 1600s, they just assumed that atoms and molecules were made up of solid particles. If you look at quantum physics that was developed during the early 1900s, there aren't any "particles." Energy is the backbone of all reality. Every particle is thought of as a vibration. Electrons will vibrate in an electron field. Protons will vibrate in the proton field. Since everything is energy, this means that all things are connected to everything else. On an elementary level, matter won't show up as particles that are isolated. All matter is a dynamic connected tissue that is vibrating energy fields. Solid matter and atoms are made up of mostly empty space; it's the same out in deep space. There is the same amount of sand on all the beaches as there are stars in the Universe. These are infinitely large numbers but in between these are all that empty space. All that unused space is wasteful. Scientists in quantum theory found that particles contain energy as well as the space that is in between everything. This is called zero-point energy. This makes the statement: "Everything consists of energy."

Zero Point Energy

Scientists have discovered there is more than just primary energy that works in the whole Universe and connects all things to all things out there. This energy was measured by Dr. Harold Puthoff first. This experiment was done at zero degrees Kelvin which are known as absolute zero. If you boil anything by adding energy to it, the molecules begin to move faster and faster. For example, when you heat water, it begins to boil and then evaporates. The opposite of this happens when you freeze water. The molecules begin to move slower, and then the water will become solid when it freezes. According to an old scientific method, no elementary particle, atom, or molecules can move an absolute zero. This means at this temperature, and it shouldn't be possible to measure energy at all. Rather than finding no energy, he found an abundance of energy that he called "a boiling witch's cauldron."

Energy That Has A Thousand Names

The science community has just recently figured out what the ancient culture has known for thousands of years, and that is energy can penetrate matter. All things come from energy, and then it returns to that same energy. This is the source of all life forms. Every culture gave it a name, and this is where it got the name: "The energy with a thousand names." You might be wondering what this is. Well, simply, it is life energy. Life energy has been known to every culture since ancient times, and each culture has a special name for it. The Chinese call this Chi. The Greeks called it Pneuma. It is known as spiritus Vitalis in Latin. It is called Prana in yoga. It is known as mana to the Kahunas in Hawaii. It is the Christian's Light. It is the ki of Reiki and the Ka of the ancient Egyptians. In today's culture, you will encounter this energy as the orgone of Wilhelm Reich, the od of Reichenback, the aether of anthroposophy, and the fluids of mesmerists. They are talking about universal, subtle energy that can penetrate and include all things in each case. This energy is what carries life and connects everything. It forms matter.

Life energy is normally mentioned with life force. It has magnetic and healing properties.

Information and Energy

All energy fields contain information. You can compare this to scripts that actors use to keep themselves organized. This field informs matter, and these turn into matter. It is similar to incarnation, where a person's soul manifests itself into another form. The information does the same thing. It turns into a form. In order to read a book, you have to digest the information and then act on what you have read; you are going to need energy.

Many people treat information and energy as if they were the same thing, and this causes a lot of misunderstanding. You have to realize that information and energy are two totally different properties. A newscaster gives information to us. If we have problems hearing them, we turn up the volume. In this moment, you are adding energy; this won't change the news or the information. You need to exert energy to get the information from the speaker out to the audience but the information will stay the same. Nobody would think that you are telling a different story if you started speaking louder. You can buy a book about anything but if you don't read the book, you won't get any information from it. Once you have read it, you will need to use energy and time to act on the things you have read.

CHAPTER 2

THE MOST COMMON MONEY BLOCKS

When it comes to money, some people believe it makes the world go round, while others think it's the root of all evil. However, you see it, money and the accumulation of wealth has always been the subject of a myriad of judgments and personal projections. Since money seems to be such a taboo subject, it's no wonder why so many people hold limiting beliefs or blocks when it comes to money. These blocks come in many shapes and sizes.

These blocks can be so deep in our psyche that they are hard to spot. In fact, there are people out there who have been manifesting and using the law of attraction for months or years and still, struggle to attract abundance. The main reason they still struggle is that they are unknowingly thwarting their own success and intentions. Before you think we only have these blocks when it comes to money, we don't. We have blocks and limiting beliefs about everything in our life, but our money blocks tend to be what causes us the most trouble.

That's why we are going to go over some of the most common money blocks people have. You may not have all of these; most people don't. There is a good chance, though, that you will have more than one. It's okay. You can learn to overcome them, and the rest of the book will help to teach you how to do just that.

1. "I don't deserve to have money."

This is a common belief for anybody who grew up in a household hearing how abundance only happens to certain people. This has caused you to develop the belief that since you aren't already rich, you don't deserve to be rich. This one tends to be one of those beliefs that you don't even realize you have because it can be so insidious. Most of the time, it's formed by simply comments that your parents or grandparents made that didn't seem that important. Unfortunately, those comments were important, and they have now shaped your mind to think you shouldn't have money because you aren't "special."

The first thing you have to do is get rid of this idea that only certain people deserve money and success. Everybody should have the chance to be as successful as they want to be and in their own way.

2. "It's not my responsibility."

This plays into the first one, but if you believe that somebody else should be financially responsible for you, then you will have problems attracting money. This person could be a spouse, partner, relative, or even the state. This belief that you are not responsible for your financial wellbeing is giving away your power. You are handing the power you have to be your own resource over to some external source that will be in charge of your finances.

This is normally caused by the belief that you don't have what it takes to be your own source of power and support. Try to spot who you might be giving your financial power to. Underneath that, try to spot any beliefs that underpin this. Do you think you aren't smart enough, or not experienced enough to deal with your money?

3. "Money only causes problems," or "Money is the root of all evil."

Abundance is a common goal for most people, but a lack of wealth can cause negative thoughts about money. While money can't fix all of our problems, dwelling on the negatives will only keep you from reaching your goals. To that end, we are often taught growing up the money will only create more problems for us. Like there is this force that once you have extra money to get to do things you want to do, some evil force is going to pop out of the earth and create problems for you. Let's look at that second quote for a second. Did you know that "money is the root of all evil" is not even the entire quote?

The quote comes from the *Bible*, specifically 1 Timothy 6:10. It actually states, "For the love of money is the root of all evil." That quote that gets thrown around so much is telling you not to be greedy. That's very different than simply having money. You could have all the money in the world and not be greedy.

Take a moment to write out all of the negative messages you have ever heard about money. This could have come from society, TV, your family, or your friends. Next to each of those statements, write down a corresponding positive belief.

4. You take cues from your environment.

Is your work or home environment subconsciously turning your mind into a vibration of lack instead of abundance? This could mean that small amounts of change are just lying around and not in an appropriate place. Your receipts could be poorly organized, or you could have a bunch of old receipts stuffed into your purse or the ashtray in your care. You could also be surrounded by things that remind you of some of your hardest times. The best thing you can do is to change the environment and get rid of those negative things. This will then reframe your thoughts.

5. You are blind to the signs.

This is a very common block. Most people use to tuning out or ignoring their gut instincts, and this attitude becomes ingrained into a person's subconscious. However, this means that you are going to miss out on the signs from the Universe that are trying to guide you towards your wealth. The next time something happens and your gut tells you to go for it, you should think about listening.

6. You have an excessively giving mindset.

Being generous and giving is great, but to manifest abundance for yourself, you have to be the giver and receiver. Are you asking the Universe to bring you wealth and then turning away what it gives you? Your worth is not only defined by what you can give to others. It is positive, healthy, and your right to want things for yourself as well. In the long run, it tends to be more beneficial if you save and act more frugal so that you can really help people in the future.

7. You lack any type of specificity.

You may think that you have a crystal clear intention for what you want to attract. What a lot of people don't realize is that the subconscious mind can push them towards setting very vague goals that they can't visualize, which makes them hard to attain. This need to be vague could be due to many things, such as being afraid of change or of the unknown. But you have to move out of this fear and really come up with a clear and concrete goal. Be specific about the amount of money you want and how soon you want it to reach you. Specificity is what will get you results.

8. You have set low expectations for yourself.

These expectations could be about your ability to gain abundance or your faith in the manifesting process. Still, a mind full of doubts won't be able to harness the energy needed to have an abundant life. To make sure that you attract what you want, you need to release your doubt. Reading manifestation success stories can be a great way to boost your vibrations and your trust in the process.

9. You are afraid of success.

It could be that your subconscious mind is afraid of getting what it wants. You may be afraid of change, or you are worried that your success won't last. While being cautious can be very beneficial, if it turns into a full-blown fear, it will end up holding you back. To deal with this, write down all of the anxieties you have towards being successful. For example, you could be worried you still won't be happy or that you aren't responsible enough to have all of that money. Then with each of those worries, write down a positive to the anxieties. Instead of, "I'm not responsible with money," try, "I know how to handle my money, responsibly."

With that said, we are also going to take a look at some common mistakes people make when they try to manifest things into their life. These mistakes can create problems for your manifestation, just like the limiting beliefs and blocks we have discussed. I think it's really important to realize the pitfalls you could wind up in before you start manifesting so that you can prevent them from happening to being with.

10. You don't create a proper intention.

An intention is what you cultivate and form in your mind that helps stimulate the law of attraction. Energy and content are the biggest parts of your intention. Content is all of the information about what you want to attract. You could want to attract money for a new house, new clothes, vacation, new car, whatever. It also works for things other than money as well, like a relationship or career. These are all different pieces of content for your intention.

The energy is the push that helps your content come to life. It helps to power up the intention and stimulate the manifestation process. That's why it's so important that you have the content and energy you need to get what you want. One won't work without the other.

11. You try to start out too big.

When you are first learning about manifestation, it is very tempting to immediately try to bring about your wildest dream, like getting a million bucks, retiring young, or finding an amazing relationship. However, the biggest dreams are typically the ones that are the furthest away from our vibrations. This is why these big dreams see feel unbelievable.

Trying to reach an "almost unbelievable" dream can be very hard. This isn't because it can't be done or hard for the Universe to give you, but instead, it's because you don't believe that it could ever actually happen. If you can't believe that it is able to happen, it won't end up happening. You have to find a way to believe that it is going to happen.

12. You say "no" when something comes your way.

I have an anecdote for you. A man is stuck in flood, and he starts praying to get rescued. A truck comes by and asks if he needs help, but the man sends him away by saying, "God will save me." Then a helicopter shows up, but the mean sends him away in the same manner. Then a boat pulls up beside him, and he, once more, sends them away. Unfortunately, the man ends up drowning because he never got rescued. When he gets to heaven, he asks God why he didn't help him. God tells him that he sent three people and asks the man why he didn't accept their help.

You can't expect to get something for nothing. You can't say, "I want a million dollars," and then sit on your couch, expecting it to show up. You can start listening and paying attention to opportunities and chances that come your way. You have to take inspired action and listen to your intuition.

13. You forget to pay attention.

There have been a lot of people who have asked for things, but they end up forgetting what they asked for in the first place. This means that they end up missing out on the opportunity when it comes to. People so often miss out on opportunities because they are not paying attention. They didn't notice when somebody said something to them that could have led them to where they wanted to be. You must make sure that you stay conscious if you are going to get what you want.

14. You end up limiting the Universe.

When you create your intentions, you shouldn't try to limit how the Universe can bring those things to you. If you would like to be able to afford to go to some type of class, you have to make sure that you remain open to all possibilities of how this can happen. Somebody could give you the money, you earn money for it, you get a scholarship, work-study, what have you, but you don't want to say, "I want to have the money to pay for this class." It is better if you keep it simple and stick with, "I want to attend this class." When the Universe is limited by your intention, you are making it harder to get the things that you want. Be as specific as you must be in order to get the things that you want.

15. You only "hope" that things are going to work out.

Your manifestation works through your intentions. Things will only work if you truly believe that they are going to work. If you simply hope that something is going to work, then you believe that there is a good chance that they won't work out.

16. You reject blessings.

People ask to get their dream career, but when they are given a job offer, they turn it down because it isn't exactly what they wanted. What they don't realize is that job could have been the stepping stone they need in order to reach their dream job. Or, while at that job, they could have met somebody that would have helped them reach their goals. In order to fix this, even if you don't believe it is what you wanted to attract, you need to realize that it could lead you to where you want to be. So you need to accept it and be grateful for it. The Universe has your best interests in mind, so you need to trust it and allow it to guide you in order to reach your desires.

17. You don't share or give what you want.

This may seem to contradict what I said in the blocks about being too giving, but hear me out. The law of attraction works by giving you want you to give out. That means if you're negative, you will attract more negative things. For example, if you want to attract love, you need to give love. This could simply mean being nice to people and not gossiping so much. If you want to attract money, you can give a bit. The difference here is, don't give so much that you take away from what you need and want. Just give a couple of dollars, or even a few cents if that is all you can afford.

18. You don't do it enough.

There are people who only say their affirmations or visualize things when they are able to remember to do so or when they "feel" like it. They don't stay consistent with their manifesting work. To fix this, you have to be repetitive. You must visualize, go through affirmations, and all of your other manifesting rituals each and every day. The best times to do these things are right when you get up and right before bed. You can also do these while waiting in line at the grocery, brushing your teeth, washing dishes, bathing, and pretty much anytime you have a chance to.

19. Your desires aren't connected with your values.

You aren't going to make money if you prefer hanging out with friends who never budget. Likewise, you aren't going to lose weight if you prefer the pleasure of eating at a buffet. To fix this, take some time to write out all of your values and then compare those values to the goals and desires you have to see if you have any conflict between them. If there is a bit of a discrepancy, know that it is going to be a lot harder to manifest your desires, and it would be better if you change your goals so that they match up with your values.

20. You refuse to take any action.

This ties into several of the other points we've talked about. There are some who choose to wish, but they never do what is necessary to get them to their goals. There are two things you can do to take action. First, start acting the part. This doesn't mean you should spend money that you don't actually have. What you can do, though, is a walk in the footsteps of a rich person. It doesn't cost anything to test drive a car or to tour a nice house. This will put you in the mindset of what you are looking to become. You can also start mingling with wealthy people.

Second, you need to take inspired action. Remember the man and the flood. You have to start paying attention to the chance events and listening to your inner voice. Don't brush it off as coincidence.

21. You blame other people for your problems, or make excuses.

When things don't turn out right or if something goes wrong, they will blame somebody else or their surroundings, or they come up with a bunch of excuses like not having the time or having too much on their plate. In order to fix this, you must take responsibility for your own life. If you are constantly making excuses or placing blame on somebody else, you are pushing away your own power. When you decide to claim that you are responsible for what happens to you, you show the Universe that you are the one in control of your own life and that you are able to turn whatever you want into your reality.

22. You word your affirmations wrong.

If your goal is to lose weight, you won't be able to reach that goal with the affirmations, "I'm not fat," or "I will be sexy." In order to fix this, you have to make sure that your affirmations are positive in the present tense. They also have to feel right. When you say something like, "I'm not fat," it is a negative statement. "I will be sexy" is not stated in the present tense, but in the future tense. This also shows that there is possibly a limiting belief about their ability to get fit. An effective affirmation for this goal would be something similar to, "I am sexy" This is positive, present tense, brief, and it isn't working against their limiting belief. It is also important that you commit to a healthy lifestyle, but this affirmation can keep you moving in the right direction.

23. You wait until the right time.

If you want to attract things, you have to think and feel good. There is something that quite a few people do, and that is, they wait for something good to happen before they start to think and feel positive. This is why they end up attracting more negative thoughts and emotions. You have to feel good now.

24. You try to resist what your current life is like.

There are some people who just can't accept what is going on right now. They are impatient, and they expect things to happen to them immediately. They feel bad that they don't have what it is that they want right now. In order to fix this, you must learn to appreciate everything that you have right now. You should dream big and do all of your manifesting rituals, but you must also be patient and never start feeling desperate to reach what you want. It is going to come to you in divine timing. Allow the Universe to come up with the "how" and "when."

25. You are always changing your mind.

One minute they want to manifest their own startup, the next, they want to be a restaurant tycoon. All this does is confuse the Universe, and it weakens your manifesting abilities. To fix this, before you even start to manifest something, make sure you know exactly what it is that you want. Create a checklist of all of your desires. Work through the checklist and figure out what your heart's true desires are. Once you have figured out exactly what it is that you want, don't switch it up unless you absolutely have to.

With all of that out of the way, you can keep an eye on your journey and make sure you aren't making any of these mistakes if you do find that you fall into some of these mistakes, which many will, you will have a good idea as to how to get yourself back on track.

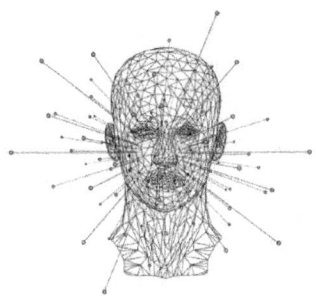

CHAPTER 3

THE SUBCONSCIOUS MIND

If you are serious about changing your life, then you have to make sure that you change your subconscious mind as well. The reason for this is the fact that the subconscious mind is always working. You could view this as autopilot, or the background noise that is taking place behind the scenes. This could also be seen as your foundational belief system because this is where all of your previous experiences have been stored in things like skills, memories, beliefs, situations you've faced, and images you've seen. The scientists who study the mind have said that as much as 95% of our decisions and actions come from this subconscious mind, not the conscious mind. The conscious mind only controls about five percent of the cognitive activities we have, like behavior, actions, emotions, and decisions.

We know that from a law of attraction perspective, what you focus is the things you will get in life. This focus you have to have is subconscious and conscious in nature. The power within your subconscious mind is able to help you reach new success in your life.

Since we already know that the subconscious mind controls 95% of our autopilot belief system, you can see that most of what you attract in life is from the vibrational energy coming from your subconscious thoughts.

This is your subconscious energy. It comes from the thoughts that are stored away in the subconscious mind. This is the main reason why people feel like they are stuck in a rut even when they consciously try to start changing their focus.

Each time you focus on something, it will become ingrained into your subconscious. The more you focus on that, the more momentum you will create in that area, and the more you will start to attract things with a similar vibration. For example, when you were a child, if you saw one of your parents cheating on the other, you probably have some strong emotions connected to that. What you saw, as well as the emotional response to it, is stored in the subconscious. When you become an adult, that memory is still within your subconscious, and while you were growing up, if you fed that energy with a mistrust of people in relationships, then you have a better chance of attracting those types of relationships into your life.

Another good example would be lack. As a child, if the environment you grew up in was always filled with an energy of lack when it came to money, then this trigger has been stored in the subconscious. Then, in your adulthood, when it comes to thinking about money, you constantly think about this lack because this was what was programmed into your mind as a child.

As you can see, the subconscious is extremely powerful, and as such, if you are looking to invoke more sustainable changes within your life, you will have to take the time to change your subconscious. When you make a point of changing your subconscious thoughts, you will begin attracting a different reality. For example, if violence has been a big part of your life, when you switch up your focus to something like peace, you will begin to see more peace over time.

This doesn't mean that you won't ever experience conflict in life anymore. It just means that you are going to be more inclined towards peace. When you make a point of changing your subconscious, you are basically shedding away old layers of beliefs and thoughts that aren't serving you and bringing out the new you. This new you is going to take on many forms, depending on the old layers that you shed. While you are shedding these various layers of conflict, you will naturally start to attract from the layer you have reached.

Let's take a look at an example. Let's say that there are ten layers of skin that you need to work through to become that peaceful person you so long to be. Now, you have only started working on that subconscious mind, and you have only been able to shed away one layer of skin. Now you have nine layers before you reach peace. Therefore, you will attract or be pulled to situations, people, and places that also have nine layers to reach peace. Now, being at nine layers is better than being at ten, but you probably won't be able to tell much of a difference between them since they are so close together.

Now, you continue to work on your subconscious mind for six months and you have managed to shed seven layers of skin, so you are now three layers away from peace. Again, you will start to attract people, situations, and places that are three layers away from peace as well. This means that the things you liked when you were at a nine no longer feel all that great right now. For example, the music that you liked to listen to might not resonate with you anymore. It could feel like the words within it create too much conflict, and since you don't resonate at that level anymore, it doesn't make you feel good. This is perfectly natural.

The Power of the Mind

The mind is a powerful being. It is a lot like a huge computer, maybe the best computer ever that is able to store and process every little thought we have. It also does a bunch of other stuff at the same time. Just like with a computer, there are some parts that you can see and work with directly and a much bigger part in the background and unseen. And whenever that background part gets broken or misaligned, we find trouble.

The conscious mind controls your awareness of your surroundings, your current emotions and thoughts, the sensations within your body, whether you're hungry, and so on. This is the part that is easy to understand. It is logical, intelligent, and commanding. The role the conscious mind plays in manifesting is quite simple. It is the part that has to decide on what you want and how you are going to get it.

The subconscious, on the other hand, takes orders from the conscious mind. This is a good thing because the subconscious is a lot more powerful than your conscious mind, but it is made up of a raw power that learn through repetition. If you repeat something enough times, the subconscious will understand that, "Okay, this is repeating, so that must mean it is important. I'll take this as true from this point on."

Basically, the subconscious doesn't really know the difference between right and wrong. It doesn't make any judgments, and it definitely doesn't understand the past and future ideas. To it, everything only exists now, and the most priority is given to the things that have the most impressive. This makes the subconscious stubborn. It will gladly take the orders of the conscious mind, but only if it agrees with the underlying logic. If the things the subconscious has learned to be true doesn't match up with the order from the conscious, you can say bye-bye to that happening. It could even end up breaking the machine in the process.

What Is In My Subconscious?

How can you find out what you have in your subconscious mind? There are many different ways to figure out, or get a good idea of, what is going on within your subconscious. The easiest way to look at the things you have manifested. What is the main energy of your current world? For example, when it comes to relationships, what type of person do you often attract into your life? Do you have friends that are honest and trustworthy? Or are they backstabbing and two-faced? Do have a lot of positive situations in your life? Do you attract situations where you tend to feel like you're the victim? Whatever your main subconscious thought system is will reflect in the things around you.

Another good way to figure out what is going on in your subconscious is to listen to the residual noise that you have in your head. For example, if you tend to have thoughts of lack of confidence, you are going to "hear" those thoughts passing through your head a lot. The caveat being that sometimes beliefs have become so much of what you have created yourself to be, that it will manifest things so consistently and quickly that you won't have the time to realize what is happening. This means that you will need to "awaken" in order to hear it.

One example may be quickly-made decisions. These are those decisions that get made so quickly that you weren't even consciously aware of the vibrations underlying the decision. Let's say that you constantly make decisions based on your lack of confidence. These types of decisions happen so often and quickly that you probably don't even realize that this is your belief system.

These decisions are so ordinary and common for you that you might not realize that they are coming from fear. Since they happen so fast, you would have to look back at decisions after you made them. For example, you would have to take the time to reevaluate most of the decisions you made during the past week.

Overcoming The Subconscious Blocks

The problem with the subconscious is that it grabs hold of anything that is repeated in your life. This means, it doesn't even have to be something you are doing to yourself. It can come from society and your family. If you grew up hearing things like, "You're fat, dumb, and lazy, and will never amount to anything," then the subconscious mind believes that to be true, even though it isn't. Unfortunately, there are quite a few of us who have been faced with such problems.

And while it is easier said than done, you need to forget everything that you've been told because you are worthy of everything you want. Everything you want, you deserve to have. You deserve everything that you desire. The fact that you are alive, you can take part in the infinite abundance of life. The corporations, media, religions, and institutions have convinced everyone that we aren't good enough. You might have even started to believe that you aren't good enough. Maybe you think you aren't worthy. You might be thinking you aren't smart enough. You have messed up so much in the past and this means you aren't allowed any freedom, success, abundance, and joy that the world offers you just because you messed up, you committed a sin, you were raised a certain way, or because you made a mistake.

You might be thinking that your legs are too skinny or your butt's too big. You might think you aren't good or smart enough. You might not think you have a good memory. Well, this is all bullshit. It has been designed to control us through the media, institutions, or religions so that we buy their things that we know we don't need and doesn't have any relevance except for a small level of satisfaction that soon fades. This is all nothing but social control.

If you don't believe that you are smart and good enough, you will be controlled. I am trying to tell you that you are worthy. So say this to yourself: "I am worthy of everything I desire." Say it again and again and again. This needs to be ingrained into your brain. Say it again: "I am worthy of everything I desire."

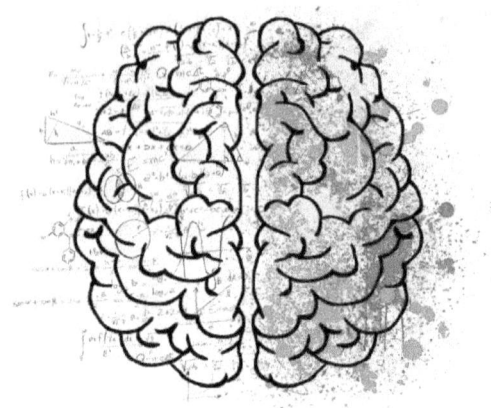

Creating a Positive Mindset

You have probably heard someone described as being either negative or positive. The truth of the matter is that we have a choice as to whether or not we want a positive mindset. It isn't a natural-born trait. You are already able to change your attitude. When you commit to this change, it will help to bring you a life that is more successful and happier.

The following steps are able to help you have a more positive outlook.

1. Act Like a Positive Person

If you are able to act like a positive person, you will be able to change your attitude and you will slowly start to change how you view the world.

Studies have shown that making yourself smile could actually change your mood. Plus, if you act like a confident person, it will make a change in your self-esteem.

When you pass a stranger, try not to use any negative adjectives. Carry yourself as if you are having the best day of your life, and be friendly by talking to others.

When you are at home, try surrounding yourself with motivational objects and positive images that make you feel inspired and content.

2. Be Appreciative

Taking five minutes each day to cultivate your appreciation, you can change up your mindset drastically. You can keep a journal close for this exercise, and just write down five things that happened during the day that you appreciate. You can write down whatever makes you feel grateful or happy.

You may recall a great conversation that you had with somebody you care about. You might have noticed a beautiful butterfly in nature or you might have gotten that raise you asked for.

While this activity is simple, it is extremely powerful because it can turn a negative mood into an optimistic mood.

3. Focus on the Present

The majority of negative people have part of their mind in the past and the other part in the future. They always dwell on regrets from their past and worry about how their new problems are going to work themselves out.

The main key to create a positive mindset is to stay focused on the present. You have to allow yourself to experience the little things. Once you begin doing this, it will be easier to appreciate all the little pleasures like showing a pet affection, going for a nature walk, or sliding between cool sheets.

Most people like performing mindfulness activities because it helps them to live in the present. It is easy to start by setting aside a bit of time to help clear out your mind and focus on your breathing.

4. Find Influences that are Positive

It can be hard to remain positive if you are constantly around people who always see the worst in everything, criticize, and complain. These attitudes are very infectious and people who constantly keep this type of mindset might make fun of you when you attempt to have a positive mindset.

Because of this, it is very important that you pick friends wisely and only surround yourself with those who provide you with optimism, support, and energy. When you socialize with these types of people, it will help to boost your spirit and provide you with a lot of things to appreciate.

5. Be Nice to Yourself

It is important to know that sharing positivity with other people doesn't mean that you have to place all your resources on selfless pursuits. Being successful and happy will involve commitment in order to meet all of your needs.

You can't be positive if you are always drained and exhausted. You should never feel guild when you turn down an invitation if you really need to recharge you batteries. You should also make sure that every day you take the time to be kind and do at least one random act of kindness towards yourself. This might seem selfish, but it's not. The only person you can guarantee on doing something for you and is yourself. It might be sleeping in, reading your favorite book again, listening to your favorite song, or fixing a sensible meal. Knowing that you deserve care and love is a major part of having a positive mindset.

You have just read seven ways to create a positive mindset, but we are going to take that a step further and look at how to declutter the subconscious mind and get rid of all those things holding you back. The subconscious is made up of "neural pathways" that have been created through conditioning and your past.

Neural pathways are links within the brain. These are very real, and they aren't all that different from a sturdy piece of rope that is created by weaving several pieces of strings together. When you can consciously see through the negativity, the neural pathway it is connected to will start to come down, but it is going to take some time. It can take months for a neural pathway to be completely taken down.

There are a lot of people who realize certain truths, and will gain clarity. But then they end up feeling frustrated that the brain can't seem to match up all of their new understanding. The problem here is that the conscious mind had learned something new, but the subconscious mind hasn't been programmed with this new belief yet.

The conscious mind is able to pick it up immediately, and you will start to feel this sense of elation and relief, but the next day you will likely face that same subconscious block that will create the old thought patterns. When you don't fully understand how the subconscious mind works, you can easily begin to beat yourself up for feeling like you're "slow," or for regressing into negativity after just only a day of being enlightened, and this only reinforces your old patterns of negativity.

Taking Down Those Neural Pathways

In order to program your subconscious with your present "conscious" understanding, it is going to take time, and you will have to make an allowance for it. Understand that this works as a physical process.

In fact, your pathways are constantly being reinforced through your life right now because your life is simply a web that has been created through thoughts. So you are going to have to create a rift in this subconscious reinforcement by consciously working to dis-identify with the negativity.

This idea of dis-identification can be confusing to some, but all it means is that you quit buying into the negativity. For example, let's say that you have managed to make a disconnected reality for yourself through different negative thought patterns that are within your subconscious mind. Now you have become conscious of this problem and you would like to get out of this pattern so that you are able to have a positive reality. The brain, though, will subconsciously try to reinforce this negativity because of the neural pathways. It is a lot like a living being needing food to survive.

Look at it like this, a smoker becomes addicted to nicotine because their brain has gotten use to its presence, even after only a few months of smoking, and the brain now believes it is necessary to survive. Once the person is no longer smoking, and the stop cold turkey, that sudden absence of nicotine will cause the brain to start to panic because it is no longer getting what it feels it needs. This is going to create a very strong sense of survival fear and it will end up taking several weeks of the abstinence from the nicotine before your brain can adjust to not receiving the nicotine on a regular basis.

It's the same thing when it comes to negativity. The brain has become so use to a specific negativity pattern that when you no longer identify with it, you will be faced with a period of withdrawal. There are a lot of reasons why staying in a space of relaxed awareness helps to bring down patterns of negativity.

1. You are able to stay relaxed. You will remain consciously relaxed instead of panicking with your brain's negative cycle; this helps to ensure that that your natural vibrations are one of fearlessness, or open. This helps to make sure that you aren't fueling your negativity, which will break the cycle.

2. You allow your mind noise. You aren't constantly trying to sort out the noise of your brain. Instead, you simply allow it. This ensures that

you don't buy into the loop of trying to fix the mind's problems with a bunch of the same patterns of thinking that caused it. This state of allowing helps you to connect with your inner being. This helps you to find real solutions and understanding so that you can bring about a lasting transformation.

3. You will become more responsive and less reactive. You will develop that ability of being able to consciously hold a space between how your brain reacts and its awareness. This ability, as it continues to grow, is what will allow you to start feeling free from being a prisoner in your own mind.

4. You will begin to understand your mind better. When you create stability within this space of awareness, you will start to understand that your mind isn't such a "big deal." It is simply a

machine that you can work with, instead of fearing it. You will realize that you have to understand your mind, learn about its natural makeup, and match up with it. You will do this while releasing negativity and resistance that keeps you from living your own life.

When you stay in a relaxed awareness, it will automatically reprogram the subconscious mind in order to align with your conscious understanding. This is due to the fact that your awareness holds the conscious understanding and making sure you stay in a space of awareness will allow you to let go of reinforcing negative patterns and to register this conscious understanding into the subconscious, thus creating new neural pathways.

So in order to help you reprogram your subconscious, let's look at some simple tasks you can undertake.

Find What Your True Purpose Is

This first thing you need to do is to figure out what your true purpose is. All I want you to do is to list out a bunch of things that spark joy and passion in you. Don't think too much about this. Just write down whatever it is that you love to do or that excites. And don't feel bad if it doesn't align with your current life. Then, to take things a step further, you will look at the qualities you prefer to express. Take a moment to think about the qualities that you love to share with the world. This can be things like joy, love, happiness, and so on. Then, write down the ways in which you like expressing these qualities. This is going to be more difficult than the last task, but there is a reason for that.

To help with this, you can take some time to meditate. I want you to look back at your past tasks and figure out where things overlap. Come up with a life purpose based on your other journaling.

Your subconscious mind does a lot better if you make sure it knows exactly what you want, and this will help you do this. Remember, it probably won't take hold in a single day. It helps if you write down what it is that you want, and hang this up somewhere in your home so you will see it several times throughout the day.

Come Up With A Visual Representation

To help reinforce the new beliefs that you want to have, you should try to create a visual representation of them. There are several ways to do this, and which one you choose will depend on how creative you want to be. The most popular options are vision boards and a mindmap. A vision board simply requires you to tape up some visual representations of things that you will like to bring into your life. A mindmap is a bit more complicated. Let's take a quick look at how to make one.

- In the center, state your "why." This is your big goal, what you would like to do. This could be something like traveling around the world and getting to stay in nice hotels without thinking about. You can list up to five things in your "why" section. This should tie into your life purpose. It is best to stick with "whys" that work together. Instead of listing health, money, and career items into one, focus on just health or just money and career.

- Right below your "why" write out your rewards. These are things you are going to give yourself as you reach your goals. These can be big or small. Maybe you have always wanted to go on a cruise, so one of your rewards could be a seven-night cruise. Out next to these rewards, you should eventually list how soon you want to be able to do them, so in three years, a couple of months, something like that.

- Draw four diagonal lines shooting off from your "why." The top right should be your "three-year goals." The top left should be your "lifetime goals." The bottom right should be your "three-month goals." The bottom left should be your "one-year goals."

- On your "lifetime goals," write down the big goals that you want to achieve over your lifetime. A lot of people want to have financial abundance. Others may want to have a multi-million dollar business. Whatever you want to achieve in your life, write it down here. And one piece of advice I have is if you want to be financially abundant, make sure you write it as such. A lot of people like to write down what they want to be financially free, and I can see what they are doing, but I have a problem with using the word free. To me, free should be put with things that you want to get rid of. For example, saying you want to be debt-free. That's why I stress you should say financially abundant. Saying you want to be financially free sounds too much like you don't want to have money.

- Then move onto your "three-year goals." This is your first step at breaking your goals down into smaller steps. Look at your "lifetime goals" and figure out where you would like to be with those goals in three-years time. Maybe in three years you have gotten your business up and running. You could have a few passive income streams. Or you could have written your first book. Write down what you know you can do in three years to get you closer to your life goals.

- Then move to your "one-year goals." You're going to be breaking those three-year goals down into smaller goals. What can you achieve in one year that will bring you closer to your three-year goals? This could be getting that promotion you want. Maybe losing 30 to 50 pounds. Creating a better relationship with your boss or co-workers. Anything that will bring you closer to your three-year goals.

- Then move onto your "three months goals." These are things you can reach in three months that will bring you closer to your one-year goals. This could include reading books and learning more about your career. You could start looking at schools if you need to go back to school for what your main goals are.

Use Affirmations

The last option for reprogramming your subconscious mind that we will go over is using affirmations. Affirmations give your subconscious mind the repetition it needs to program this new truth into it. It is best if you create your own affirmation, but there are a lot of pre-written affirmations you can find online that you can use.

When writing your own, make sure that you use the present tense. You also want to make sure that your affirmation is positive. This means that you should not write an affirmation using a negative word like don't or doesn't. The subconscious mind doesn't pay attention to that. You should only focus on what you want. Lastly make sure it is short and uses power words.

CHAPTER 4

CREATING A MONEY MINDSET

Any negative things you have been told during your life, you need to forget about them right now. You are worthy of having the best life you could dream of, and you can achieve whatever you want. Everything you want, you deserve to have. There are lots of people out there who say, "Oh, well, I don't deserve that two-story farmhouse that I've dreamed of since childhood, that vintage '69 Corvette, that promotion I've had my eye on, and the money I would like to make."

You deserve everything that you desire. The fact that you are alive, you can take part in the infinite abundance of life. The corporations, media, religions, and institutions have convinced everyone that we aren't good enough. You might have even started to believe that you aren't good enough. Maybe you think you aren't worthy. You might be thinking you aren't smart enough. You have messed up so much in the past and this means you aren't allowed any freedom, success, abundance, and joy that the world offers you just because you messed up, you committed a sin, you were raised a certain way, or because you made a mistake.

You might be thinking that your legs are too skinny or your butt's too big. You might think you aren't good or smart enough. You might not think you have a good memory. Well, this is all bullshit. It has been designed to control us through the media, institutions, or religions so that we buy their things that we know we don't need and doesn't have any relevance except for a small level of satisfaction that soon fades. This is all nothing but social control.

If you don't believe that you are smart and good enough, you will be controlled. I am trying to tell you that you are worthy. So say this to yourself, "I am worthy of everything I desire." Say it again and again and again. This needs to be ingrained into your brain. Say it again, "I am worthy of everything I desire."

This isn't anything new. This is to try and woo you. You literally deserve everything you desire. Anybody who achieves anything great, who has created anything amazing in their lives, they believe that they are worthy to have it. They aren't any more special than you. They aren't any better than anyone else. We are all worthy. We are all deserving of it.

We all deserve the best life possible. We all deserve to have happiness. We all deserve to have others treat us with respect. You deserve it, too. This means that you are allowed to say no and cut people out of your life that might not be reciprocating the support you deserve. This might mean you have to say no to things. This might mean that you have to ask for what you want but you deserve it. If you deserved everything you have ever wanted, if you are worthy of everything you want, if you are qualified for everything you want and you are ready, then there isn't any more prep work you need, you don't have to have your sins cleansed, you don't have to have your energy cleansed, everything has already been done. What would you do?

What things would you create? What would you do in the next year for it to be the most fulfilling and successful year of your life? What things do you really deserve? What is it that you really want for yourself, your community, your family? What?

If there aren't any more processes you have to go through to be worthy, to be a higher energy, to clean out all the processes your subconsciousness has been programmed with? If at this moment in time you were free from all the things your so-called friends told you, your hateful boss said to you, all those things your mom said to you, all that stuff your teachers told you, if all that were to magically go away, what would you do?

I am here to remind you that you are worthy of everything you want.

All you have to do is to train your subconscious mind that you are worthy of abundance and success. You have to get rid of all those silly ideas that you aren't good, worthy or smart enough. You have to erase them from your brain. You don't have to take any negativity. You don't have to take crap off anyone. You deserve whatever you want and you can move through the world with joy and peace and create an experience that you really want, not what you think you are worthy of and not what other people have told you that you are worthy of.

You deserve to have a life that is amazing and I am here to tell you that you are worthy. I am here to give you an affirmation that you need to repeat to yourself as many times per day as you can.

"I deserve everything I desire. I am worthy of everything I desire in abundance, success, happiness, and love. I deserve it. I am worthy of everything I desire."

Now, get out there with you newfound boldness and confidence. Walk with confidence toward your dreams and watch the universe respond. Claim everything you deserve and are worthy of. We live in an abundant, infinite world. There is enough for everybody to experience abundance, success, freedom, love, and joy that we want.

Why Is Mindset Important

We know that everything is energy; our body and our mind. This means our thoughts are also energy. Our thoughts are able to create an invisible force that originates within the mind. There are studies about this concept, which is known as Mind Power.

The thought that we create in our mind not only affects our personal life, but the lives of people around us. We affect people within out physical reality when we use our thoughts. Because of the law of attraction, everything that happens to us, happens because we have attracted it to us.

The most common saying you will see within law of attraction teachings is that like attracts like. It is the number one rule of the law of attraction, so let's take a deeper look as to what this means for us and how it weaves its way into our lives.

First off, I want to ask you a question. What is your work? What is it that you have to do? There is work that we all have to do in order to be able to live the phenomenal life we all deserve, but it's not the work that you would think. The work you need to do is not to "be" a certain way or to "attract." The work that needs to be done is to allow yourself to relax into divine frequency.

There is no need to try and find this frequency, it lives within you. It is within everybody, and there are no exceptions. There are common things that people do to relax into this, such as meditation and affirmations.

Now, I'm going to throw you a curve ball. There isn't anything that you have to attract because everything already exists within you. We were all created in order to interpret our own life as an experience of manifesting things that are outside of you and to bring them within. This is the reason why it is referred to as the law of attraction.

However, the truth is everything you could every want in life is already within you. There is no need to bring these thing to yourself from an outside place. If it seems that you deepest desires isn't manifesting, then you are likely keeping it away with opposing frequencies.

Everything is energy, and all of this energy comes with its own frequency. Every frequency is different, and that is the reason why everyone and everything around seems to be outside of you. However, things aren't separate, and all things are a part of the same soup of energy. When you change your frequencies to match your desires, this is when you "attract" what has always been there. Your desire, which had been invisible, has now become visible through a change in frequency. This is when you notice that you have manifested it into your physical world. The desire or dream has been there from the get go, but you had been operating on a different frequency level.

Real-Life Examples

It's easy to just tell a person we attract, or bring into our consciousness, things that match our frequency, but it's another to show them this truth in reality. So, to show you that like attracts like isn't just some saying, let's take a look at some real-life stories. This will look at the belief of like attracts like from a therapy stand point. Specifically dysfunctional relationships.

For those who have been in a relationship, it is easy to see what the other person is doing wrong, but it tends to be pretty hard to see how you may be adding to the problem. However, due to this like attracts like law, your end is the same as your partner's because we attract people that have a common level of health, a common level of woundedness, and so one.

This means that whatever degree you choose to emotionally abandon yourself, through judging yourself, turning to addictions, ignoring your feelings, or make other people responsible for how you feel, is the same degree that you partner will emotional abandon themselves.

When a person starts to criticize their partner, the person is likely criticizing their self and may be giving themselves up to their partner in order for them to get their approval. Both of them are controlling is some way, but one is only aware of how the other is controlling them. Let's say Pam says Mark is withdrawing, she is also telling you about her anger. It is two sides of their dysfunction. The issue is, Pam and Mark got together because they wanted love, instead of getting to know how to love themselves and to share that love.

Does this sound like something you want to face? While like does attract like, it does not mean you have to attract negative relationships. If you learn to love yourself, then you can attract somebody who knows how to do the same, which will create a more cohesive relationship. Let's look at what it means to attract you common level of emotional health.

To attract at your common level of emotional health means that you have worked on yourself to heal from feelings of insecurity and shame. This means that you already know how to fill yourself with love and then how to share that same love with other people. It means that you no longer abandon yourself and know how to show yourself love, which means that you know you are responsible for how you feel, instead of trying to avoid your feelings or making others responsible.

Once you have learned how to value yourself , and to take reasonability for your own feelings, you aren't going to attract a person who emotionally abandons themselves. You will, instead, attraction those who value themselves and prefers to share love instead of get love. This means you won't end up with a person who judges, withdraws, blames, or sees themselves as a victim. You aren't going to find this person attraction because they don't function on the same common emotional health level.

We know everything vibrates at different frequencies. Those on a low frequency are those who self-abandon and feel insecure. They will attract other people that vibrate on that same low frequency. People who vibrate at a high frequency are those who value and love themselves, and will attract others who feel the same. Those who are kind to themselves and others, caring, giving, secure, open, and positive will not be attracted to people who are needy of attention and approval, negative, and closed.

While most people don't deliberately look for a person who is needy, negative, and closed, if you are, this is going to be the type of person you attract into your life. If you are looking to have a functional and loving relationship, then you will have to do some work on learning how to take emotional responsibility. This will mean:

- Learning to take some form of loving action for yourself instead of expecting other people to do it.
- Learning to find your own spiritual source of love instead of expecting another person to become your higher power.

- Being open to learning more about your feelings instead of protecting yourself from them through self-judgments and addictions.
- Learning how to be present in your body instead of stuck inside you mind and trying to avoid how you feel.

This idea works in other aspects of your life as well, and working on loving yourself can help you raise your vibrations for every area of your life.

Seven Ways to Create a Positive Mindset

You have probably heard someone described as being either negative or positive. The truth of the matter is that we have a choice as to whether or not we want a positive mindset. It isn't a natural-born trait. You have all the power in the world to change your attitude. When you commit to this change, it could lead you to a more successful, happier life.

These steps will help you start your journey toward a more positive outlook.

1. Act More Positive

When a person, even if they are completely pretending, can act like a positive person, it will change their attitude and they will start to turn into that positive person. Studies have shown that making yourself smile could actually change your mood. Plus, if you act like a confident person, it can start to change your self-esteem.

When you pass a stranger, try not to use any negative adjectives. Carry yourself as if you are having the best day of your life, and be friendly by talking to others. When you are at home, try surrounding yourself with motivational objects and positive images that make you feel inspired and content.

2. Be More Appreciative

If you only had five minutes to dedicate to cultivating appreciation in your life, you could end up making drastic changes to your mindset. Make sure that had a notepad handy to do this exercise, and the write down just things that have happened during the day that you appreciate. You can write down anything that has made you happy to be where you are.

It could be that you remember a great conversation that you had with somebody in your family. A beautiful butterfly could have been following you around on your walk this morning. You may have gotten approved for a raise you asked for. This is a simple activity, but it has huge ramifications when it comes to changing your mood.

3. Focus on What is Happening Now

Many negative people live with part of them in the past and the other one in their future. They constantly dwell on regrets from their past and worry about how their new problems are going to work themselves out.

The main key to create a positive mindset is to stay focused on the present. Allow yourself to completely experience every little thing about your remarkable life. Once you begin doing this, it will be easier to appreciate all the little pleasure like showing a pet affection, taking a walk in nature, or sliding between cool sheets.

Some find that mindfulness exercises are a great way to improve their ability to enjoy their present moment. You can start out by setting some of the time aside to clear the mind and simply focus on your breath.

4. Uncover Positive Influences

It can be hard to remain positive when you are surrounded by people who always see the worst in everything, criticize, and complain. These attitudes are very infectious and people who constantly keep this type of mindset might make fun of you when you attempt to have a positive mindset.

Because of this, it is critical to pick your friends wisely and spend time with people who are supportive, optimistic, and energetic. Socializing with these people will give your spirit a boost and will give you a lot to appreciate.

5. Don't Go to the Worst Case Scenario All of The Time

It doesn't matter what you want out of life, visualize yourself achieving your goals. Never allow yourself to visualize confusion, terror, embarrassment, or failure. Rather than coming up with extremely detailed pictures of pleasure, success, and happiness, a good way to lower your tendency to always see the worst is to remind yourself that you can do anything and handle whatever come at you. With enough effort and time, any sad, stressful, or difficult ordeal can be turned into a positive experience that will secure you more success in the future.

6. Share Positive with Those Around You

Sending happiness to other people is another step toward a positive mindset. When you are nice to others, their reactions will make a feedback loop that will create a more positive feeling in you. This will then encourage you to share your positivity with others.

You don't have to do anything drastic to apply this to your life. All you have to do is be sure you compliment people when they deserve it. You might tell your cousin that she looks pretty in her new dress, thank your boss for giving you extra help on that project, remind your significant other of a reason why you feel in love with them, or congratulate a coworker on a great presentation.

All of these gestures will make others feel great and will help you reach your goal of being a more positive person.

7. Treat Yourself Nicely

It is important to know that sharing positivity with other people doesn't mean that you have to place all your resources on selfless pursuits. Being a successful, happy person involves a commitment to meet your needs.

It is impossible to remain positive if you are completely drained and exhausted. Never feel guilty for turning down invitations if you are in need of recharging your batteries.

Be sure that each day of your life involves one act of random kindness toward yourself. It might be sleeping in, reading your favorite book again, listening to your favorite song, or fixing a sensible meal. Knowing that you deserve care and love is a major part of having a positive mindset.

Like Attracts Like and Toxic Positivity

Toxic positivity isn't something that is usually talked about in law of attraction teachings, but I have found that it is important to understand that positivity can be taken too far.

First off, let's do a little experiment. When you are happy and in a good mood, how does everything and everyone around seem? When you are genuinely happy, doesn't the day seem to go smoother and everybody you are in contact with seem happy and more pleasant to be around? Now, when you are in a funk or feeling down, how does everything around you seem? It seems like everybody on the road is an idiot and can't drive. The barista doesn't spell your name right and forgets to give you the three pumps of vanilla you asked for. All of you coworkers are constantly bugging you over things that they should know how to do. This is what like attracts like means.

I also understand that sometimes you are in a good mood and something bad happens that knocks you out of it, that's life. It can become tricky, especially for people new to the law of attraction, to separate things. Some like to get caught up on the fact that we attract everything in our life. This means that whenever something bad happens, they caused it and they end up falling into a negative spiral. That's understandable because some law of attraction teachings can be quite confusing.

The only thing I can say is that bad things will happen no matter how positive you try to say, and positivity can easily become toxic. While we know that having a sunny disposition can improve your life, but it is also possible to overdose on this sweet nectar of euphemizes like "everything is awesome."

Toxic positivity is defined as "ineffective and excessive overgeneralization of a happy, optimistic state across all situations." Toxic positivity tends to cause minimization, denial, and invalidation of the true human emotions. Much like anything else that is done in excess, when positivity is used to silence or cover up the human experience, it ends up becoming toxic. When you disallow the existence of certain feelings, it causes us to fall into a state of repressed emotions and denial. In reality, humans are flawed beings. We get greedy, resentful, angry, and jealous. Sometimes life simply sucks. When you pretend to have "positive vibes all day," you are denying the validity of an actual human experience.

So, let's take a look at how to know if you are experiencing toxic positivity.

1. You are hiding or masking your true feelings.

2. Brushing things off that are bugging with the thought "it is what it is."
3. Chastising or shaming others for expressing frustration or anything that isn't positive.
4. Trying to provide a person with perspective, instead of validating how they are feeling.
5. Minimizing the experiences of others with "feel good" statements or quotes.
6. Feeling guilty for feeling how you feel.
7. Trying to "just move on with it" by dismissing or stuffing your emotions.

Toxic positivity isn't really positivity and will only attract more emotional repression and experiences that prevent you from experiencing really happiness.

First off, it creates shame. When you force a positive outlook on pain means you are encouraging a person to remain silent about what they are struggling with. Most people don't want to be viewed as a drag, so you are face with two choices. One, be honest and brave, or, two, pretend like everything is find. Most people are tempted to choose number two. Shame exists where there is denial, secrets, and hiding.

Shame cripples the human spirit and is one of the most uncomfortable feelings that you can experience. Oftentimes, we don't even realize that we are feeling shame. If you want to know if you are feeling shame, ask yourself this, "If they knew (state something about yourself) about me, what would they think?" If you are able to fill in the blank with anything, then there is a good chance you feel shame about it.

Secondly, it causes suppressed emotions. There are a lot of psychological studies that have found that denying or hiding your feels causes more stress on your body and an increased difficulty avoiding that feeling or thought. The studies they have performed on the subject has found that expressing a broad range of emotions, even ones that aren't positive, having words to express how your feeling, and facial expressions for them, helps people to regular their stress response.

When we try to not show a certain part of ourselves, we will end up creating a public persona for the outside world to see. This façade may look cheery and telling everybody "Everything happens for a reason, and it is what it is," but what you are actually doing is denying your truth. In reality, life sometimes hurts. If you are feeling angry, and you don't acknowledge them, they will get buried deep inside of you. These suppressed emotions show up later as depression, anxiety, or a physical illness.

It is very important to acknowledge the reality of your emotions by verbalizing them and getting them out of your body. This will help you to remain, healthy, sane, and relieves you are the tension that is created by suppressing your truth. Once you are able to honor how you feel, you will embrace all of yourself, the good side and the bad said. And being able to accept yourself just as you are will create a path to robust emotional life.

Third, it creates isolation and relationship problems. When you deny your truth, you start to live an inauthentic life with yourself and the world. You lose the connection with yourself, which makes it hard for others to relate with you or connect. While you might come off as unbreakable, on the inside you are scared and simply want a hug.

When you are around one of those sugary sweet people with the "just think happy thoughts" kind of attitude, do you feel at ease and like you could spill your guts to them? While that person could have the best intentions, the message they are sending is, "only good feelings can be in my presence." This makes it pretty hard to express anything but positivity around them. This will end up causing you to comply with this implied rule of , "I can only be a certain type of person around you, and I can't be myself."

The relationship you have with yourself is often seen in the relationship that you have with others. If you are unable to be honest about how you feel, how are going to be able to hold space for somebody else to express real feelings in your presence? When you create a fake emotional world, you will only attract more fakeness, which results in superficial friendships and counterfeit intimacy.

Much like having a loving relationship requires you to love yourself first, to be able to experience real positivity, you have to accept the bad feelings as well.

Before we wrap this up, here are some examples of toxic statements versus their non-toxic counterparts.

- Toxic: "It could be worse." **Accepting**: "That sucks. I'm sorry you're having to go through this."

- Toxic: "Everything happens for a reason." **Accepting**: "Sometimes we can draw the short straw in life. How can I support you during this time?"
- Toxic: "Look for the silver lining." **Accepting**: "I see you. I'm here for you."
- Toxic: "Delete negativity." **Accepting**: "Suffering is a part of life, you are not alone."
- Toxic: "If I can do it, so can you!" **Accepting**: "Everyone's story, abilities, limitations are different, and that's okay."
- Toxic: "Positive vibes only." **Accepting**: "I'm here for you both good and bad."
- Toxic: "Everything will work out in the end." **Accepting**: "This is really hard, I'm thinking of you."
- Toxic: "Failure is not an option." **Accepting**: "Failure is a part of growth and success."

- Toxic: "Don't worry, be happy." **Accepting**: "I see that you're really stressed, anything I can do?"
- Toxic: "Don't think about it, stay positive." **Accepting**: "Describe what you're feeling, I'm listening."

Begin a healthy person involves staying conscious of ourselves and how you show up in the world. If you notice that you are a transmitter of toxic positivity, you should cut it out. You are only hurting yourself, the people you care about, and your manifesting by insisting on this monochromatic mindset. Instead of trying to be positivity at all costs, aim for balance and acceptance of good and bad emotions instead of an all-or-nothing thinking.

If you have been influenced by toxic positivity, it is best to create healthy boundaries with people who passes judgment on your real experience and share your truth. We only have one chance at the imperfect, beautiful and painful life. Embrace it completely and fully and you will reap the reward of bountiful life.

CHAPTER 5

LEARNING WHAT YOU WANT

You've probably started to create a picture of what manifestation and the law of attraction looks like. But an issue a lot of people tend to have is not knowing what they want. You can't manifest things if you don't know what you want to manifest. In fact, you could be manifesting a feeling of "I don't know." When asked what you want to eat, do you say I don't know? Do you find yourself staring into your closet unsure of what you're going to wear?

Every time you say "I don't know," you are creating a world where you don't know. It doesn't matter if the words are relevant or not. As you've learned, your words create your reality. This mean you likely don't know what you want to manifest, or how much money you want. But I bet you do know what you want. You know it in every fiber of your being, but you aren't willing to admit it.

All of those thoughts and dreams that you push away because you think they aren't possible or couldn't happen, those are the things that you want to be bringing into your life. Every time they come up, they are messages from the Universe that this is where your life should be going. That's what you're going to do. You're going to sit down and think about all of those things you have pushed away and figure out what you want to manifest from those things. You can manifest all of them if you want, but let's start with only one right now.

Coming Up with an Action Plan

An action plan is what you can use to bring what you want into your life. It is important that you give your intentions legs, otherwise they can't get to you. You are not going to be handed things by the Universe, but once you start working towards your goals, the Universe is going to make sure the you get what you want. Let's take a look at the best way to create an action plan.

1. Come Up with a Visual Representation

The first thing to do in your action plan is to come up with some form of visual representation or a mindmap of your goals. To do this, you have to be crystal clear as to what your goals are. Then you break those goals down into smaller ones that you can easily accomplish. These smaller goals also need to be SMART goals. This stands for specific, measurable, actionable, and time sensitive. This ensures that you know exactly when you have achieved that goal. Let's go over creating a mindmap.

First, right in the middle of the paper state your "why." This is your big goal, the main thing that you want to accomplish. This could be something like traveling around the world and getting to stay in nice hotels without thinking about. You can list up to five things in your "why" section. This should tie into your life purpose. It is best to stick with "whys" that work together. Instead of listing health, money, and career items into one, focus on just health or just money and career.

Right below this, write out your rewards. These are things that you are going to get once you achieve your goals. You can make this rewards as big or as small as you would like. Maybe a dream of yours is to take a cruise, so a reward could be going on a cruise. It could also be smaller, like a day at the spa or going to a movie.

Out next to your rewards, you should eventually write out how soon you want to get to those things. This could be in a few years, a couple of months, or something like that.

Next, draw four diagonal lines coming off of your why. The top write is going to be your "three-year goals." The top left is going to be your "lifetime goals." The bottom right is your "three-month goals." The bottom left is your "one-year goals."

In the section for your "lifetime goals," list out your big goals that you would like to achieve during your life. Something a lot of people will put here is financial abundance. Others will say having a multi-million dollar business. Whatever you would like your life to be in the long-run, list in this space. And one piece of advice I have is if you want to be financially abundant, make sure you write it as such. A lot of people like to write down what they want to be financially free, and I can see what they are doing, but I have a problem with using the word free. To me, free should be put with things that you want to get rid of. For example, saying you want to be debt-free. That's why I stress you should say financially abundant. Saying you want to be financially free sounds too much like you don't want to have money.

Once you have that finished, you can move onto your "three-year goals." This is going to be the first step in breaking your big goals down into smaller goals. Take a look at the "lifetime goals" and figure out what is something slightly smaller than that, that you could have in three-years from now. This could be having a business up and running. You could also have a couple of different passive income streams. It could be that you have completed your first book. Write down what you know you can accomplish in three-years so that you are closer to your ultimate goals.

Then break those down further at your "one-year goals." Take those three-year goals, and make them smaller. What can you do in a single year that is going to bring your closer to the three-year goals? This could be getting a promotion. Losing some weight. Forming a closer relationship with a co-worker or boss.

Lastly, you will do your "three months goals." These are going to be things that you can accomplish in just three months time that will take you close to your one-year goals. This could be reading a book and learning more about your career. You might also go back to school if you are going to require more education for your main goal.

You now have a mindmap and you can move onto the next step in creating an action plan.

2. Create a Visual Representation of Your Daily Routine

Next, you will move onto the smaller aspects of your overall goals. This means that you can mindmap your daily action plan so that you are always working towards your goals. This will make things a lot easier for you and will keep you on track.

On a new sheet of paper, place your "one-year goals" in the middle. Just look back on your other mindmap to see what you placed in that section. Once again, draw those four lines. The top left is "strategy." Top right is "daily focus." Bottom left is "daily feel-good plan." Bottom right is "daily habits."

For "strategy," you will write down your strategy for achieving your one-year goals. This might be going back to school, take extra classes, strengthening relationships at work, daily relaxation, exercising, whatever can help you reach that goal.

Draw two lines off of that and label one "skills" and the other "mentors." In these areas, you will write down the mentors and skills that you need or want in order for the strategy to work. The mentors can be real people you know or authority figures that you want to follow. The skills will depend on what it is that you want to do.

The on "daily focus," you will write out what you would like to do every day. This might be writing in a gratitude journal, making sure you distress, work on something important, and so on.

Make two lines off of this section as well. This should be labeled, "top three actions" and "mindset." Under "top three actions" you are going to put the three things that you will make sure you do every single day. Under "mindset" write your mindset goals, like patience, compassion, positivity, and the like.

Then take a look at your "daily feel-good plant." These will be things that you are going to do each day to make sure that you feel good. These could be eating healthy, exercising, meditating, rewards, and anything else that you know will relax you. The main thing is to not list alcohol or drugs. Having a drink of wine is fine, but that should not be how you distress. It can be part of the process, like taking a bubble bath and having some wine, but the bubble bath is the de-stressor, not the wine. Turning to addictive things to feel good can lead to problems.

Lastly, fill out the "daily habits" section. These are things you are going to make a habit of doing every day. This could be saying your affirmations each morning, reading a book, spending time by yourself, visualizing success, and so on.

Now, let's move onto step three.

3. Come Up with a Monthly Action Plan

We've gone from the macro picture to the micro picture, now we are going to look at the middle of these two extremes. Before you start to plan out your monthly action plan, you need to take a look back at your one-year goals first. This is what you are striving for.

First, figure out what your goal for the next month is. Sit down and visualize yourself reaching that goal and feel grateful for having reached it. Then come up with a way to reward yourself for when you reach your monthly goal.

Next, you will need to write out your action steps or intentions that you will need to do to keep yourself feeling good and staying within a positive emotional vibration. Then list out the habits and skills that you would like to learn within that month.

Then make another list of goals that are in other areas of your life that you would like to reach during this month, and then explain why you want to reach those. You need to set a reward for each of those goals as well.

Next, list out the top five action steps that you are going to take to reach those goals. You should focus on the 20% of the tasks that are going to provide you with 80% of the results. Using a blank calendar to list out these things along with other important events, reminders, meetings, and appointments for the month is a good idea.

We are going to continue to break this down and move onto the weekly plan.

4. Come Up with a Weekly Plan

We're taking things smaller again. This will make sure that you are working, each week, to reach your monthly goals. As always look back to your one-year goals and monthly action plan before planning out your week.

Write down the goals you have for the week and then take some time visualizing yourself reaching that goal and feel grateful for having achieved it. Come up with a reward you will get for reaching that goal and picture yourself getting that reward.

Next, write down what you are going to do during the week to make sure you stay feeling good and remain in positive vibrations. Then jot down all of your to-do's that you will have for the following week. When you do this, list in order of priority and picture yourself checking off all of those tasks with ease, effortlessly, and successfully.

Then come up with your personal to-do's for the coming week, listing them in order of priority. Then picture yourself finishing all of those tasks with ease. During the week, you will want to monitor all of the new habits that you want to establish during the month. Write down when you did them, how often, and for how long.

Then go through each day and write down the goal for each day. Picture yourself reaching those goals and feel grateful for having reached them. Then write down your three most important priorities for each day. Write down your law of attraction quotes for the week to make sure you stay inspired.

As you have noticed, rewards have been mentioned several times in this section. The human brain will respond to two different things when it comes to learning and attaining new knowledge and behaviors: reward and feedback. You need to be brave enough to ask for feedback for things you are doing, and then having rewards established for each goal you accomplish will keep you motivated to do more.

CHAPTER 6

CULTIVATING GRATITUDE

There may come a time when you feel as though you won't every manifest what you want. If that be the case, then there a good chance that you aren't using the magical combination of gratitude and the law of attraction.

This is a very important step when you are trying to use the law of attraction and manifest things into your life. This is something that most people will forget about because it is so simple. They can get wrapped up in the visualization process and the creation of lists that they forget that this part is just as important as all of the rest.

Even if they do remember to use gratitude, they end up doing it wrong.

Remember, manifestation has to do with vibrations. You attract things on the same vibrational level that you are on. That means if you are feeling down, sad, depressed, or negative, you are going to attract things with those vibrations. That's why gratitude can be such a powerful tool. It can help raise your vibrations even when you are going through tough things in your life. After all, you don't want to fall into toxic positivity. You want to make sure you feel your feelings, just don't want to get stuck in that space. Gratitude can pull you out.

Fuel For Gratitude

If you would like to have a life that you are happy with, why wouldn't you fuel yourself with as much happiness as you possibly can. Everybody wants to be happy. The big question is how can we be happy? Have you been fueling yourself with happiness if you life hasn't been happy?

The answer you are looking for is gratitude fuel. This is everything and anything that you can do to help you appreciate the smallest aspects of life. When you fuel yourself with happiness, and it doesn't matter how unhappy your life might seem, it means that you have to find things that you can be grateful for as often as you possibly can.

How much gratitude fuel you use needs to be greater than all the negative aspects of your life. Basically, this is saying the worse you think your life is, the more gratitude fuel you have to give yourself each day.

Find Gratitude When Life is Rough

Each day you meet people whose lives are great and then you see people whose live could be a lot better.

The people who need a better life have something in common, they don't have the gratitude for the things they have. They can't get anything else if they don't appreciate everything they already have. Not having gratitude keeps them from getting more.

It doesn't matter how bad a person's life might be, there is always something that you can be grateful for. Once they realize this and find their gratitude, they will see an improvement in their lives.

When you complain, you are focusing your mind on what you think are problems. If the Universe understands that there aren't any problems. That everything was made by you and for you and you have the ability to change everything that you created all for the better or the worse.

If you would like to lose everything in your life, if you would like for your life to be harder, if you would like to struggle to pay your bills, if you would like to feel unloved and lose all your relationships, just keep complaining.

If you would like your life to be better in every way possible, if you would like to have more money than you can possibly spend, if you would like to have loving, wonderful relationships, if you would like to be fulfilled and happy, you just need to be grateful.

Being grateful can cause abundance. Complaining only creates poverty.

Stop being impressed by what you see around you and everything you think is wrong in your life. How you see you life is very powerful. You have to visualize you life as if it already exists. You have to visualize you life getting better in every area. You need to be joyful and feel alive as things begin to move to make you life wonderful.

You are already connected to the Universe's energy. It doesn't matter how you think your life looks, you are in control of the power that will make it better. Having this knowledge should inspire you to appreciate everything you have around you and to be grateful for the things that are coming your way.

Think about the gap between where your life is right now like physically, energetically, relationally, emotionally, and financially, it might feel extremely far away from where you would like to be.

Now, you need to begin using everything you have to notice things you can be thankful for. This means you might have to be silly about the things you appreciate. You might find there are numerous thing that you just take for granted.

If you want to completely change your life, if you want to make the law of attraction work faster, if you would like to manifest things faster, just start being grateful for everything you have. Gratitude has the ability to completely transform your life. It is powerful, simple, and fast. It has the energy to bring you immediate results.

Think about all the things that you have in your life that you can be grateful for at this present moment. You are going to be amazed at how many things you actually have. You have to be grateful for even the smallest things since having gratitude for those things can make your life a lot better than it already is.

Be sure you are grateful for the things that you are going to receive. Think about all the things that you might want to bring into your life and be grateful for it now whether it is a massage, a new car, happiness, inner peace, a new house, a boat, a vacation, a new job, money, or love.

Being grateful right now for all the things you would like to manifest tells the Universe that is you already own it and you are open to claiming it. This energized the law of attraction and this in turn enables you to manifest things faster.

Be thankful for everything you have attracted at this very moment. Allow your heart to overflow with gratitude. Each day take the time to say "thank you." You need to say this 100 times before you leave your house each morning. You can say this when you are showering. You can say it when you are brushing your teeth. You can say it when you are getting dressed. Understand that every time you say "thank you" you are creating a powerful day.

Continue saying "thank you" during the day for anything and everything that happens. By doing this, you will open yourself up to synchronicity and you will start getting more things than you ever imagined were possible.

To help you find gratitude, remind yourself of these things:

- Be thankful for the sky being clear and blue.
- Be thankful that the flowers are blooming.
- Be thankful for the comfortable sheets that you slept on last night.
- Thank the sweet old man that always smiles and says hello.
- Be thankful for the smooch you got from your pet this morning.
- Thank the cashier who gave you a coupon and help you save some money.
- Be thankful for the roof you have over your head.
- Be thankful for the clothes you have on your back.
- Be thankful for being able to take a walk around the park during your lunch break.
- Every time you drive your car, be thankful that you have one.
- Be thankful each morning that you woke up.

- Be thankful every time that you eat food.
- Be thankful every time that you get to see something in your favorite color.

If this list seems to be a bit much right now, then why don't you think about starting a gratitude journal. This is a great tool that helps you believe in your goals and your success while giving you a positive mindset. A gratitude journal is when you write everything down that you are grateful for. You need to do this each day.

Every night before you get ready for bed, write down between five and ten things that you are grateful for. When you do this, it keeps your mind positive and makes you reflect on all the good things that you have in your life. When you can concentrate on creating a happy life, you are teaching yourself to expect the most in your future. This helps you visualize your future, in meaningful and positive ways.

When you keep a gratitude journal, you can look back on all the things that you were grateful for and take as many messages and lessons from them as you can. Reflecting back on the good things about your life and yourself that you wrote in the gratitude journal can enhance your beliefs that you deserve so you can reach your goals.

Growing Your Gratitude

At the end of the day, simply writing in a gratitude journal may not help you cultivate as much gratitude as you would like or need. You should continue to write in your journal, but we are going to go over a few more ways to cultivate gratitude so that you can raise your vibrations whenever you need to.

1. Take Notice

It's important that you become aware of your negativity, complaining, or gossiping. Take notice of how you perceive the world. When you are caught in traffic, do you get angry and start yelling at the driver in front of you? Do you let the circumstances around you dictate the type of mood you are in, or can breathe and get into a place of gratitude and calmness? Think, "I am so grateful that I have this car and it will get me where I need to go despite this traffic." It's important to become mindful of how you think and feel in certain situations.

2. Change Your Point of View

After you have started to become more aware of how you act in situations, and you are keeping up with a gratitude journal, start to change your point of view from negative to positive, or upset to grateful. This is going to take some time and a lot of practice. You are the only person responsible for how you think and how you feel. That means you can create gratitude simply by saying you feel that way.

3. Look for Quality, Not Quantity

Forcing a person to be grateful does not work. This will feed the power imbalances that will end up undermining gratitude in the first place, and it can cause expressions of gratitude to feel inauthentic. The key is to form times and spaces that help to foster the spontaneous and voluntary expressions of gratitude. Studies have consistently shown that there is such a thing as too much gratitude, it seems as though trying to be grateful every single day will cause gratitude fatigue.

How can you convey authenticity? Details. When you are specific about how thing, action, or person benefits you, it increases your appreciation. It also tells a person that you are paying attention instead of just going through the motions.

4. Be Humble

The definition of humility is an "act of being modest or respectful." Think about the things you take for granted and see if you can change your attitude and position on those things. Humility will help you to be open to new ways of thinking and will change how you experience the world.

5. Share Appreciation

It doesn't hurt to give praise or a compliment for things. Let others know that you appreciate them for whatever it is that they bring into your life. Try practicing random acts of kindness and expect nothing in return. Throw out positive energy and vibes simply because you can.

6. See the Silver Lining

Start making some lemonade out of life's lemons. If you find yourself in a tough situation, ask, "what can I learn from this?" "How can I make sure that this won't happen again or how could I have reacted differently to this?"

This is particularly helpful in the workplace, as it can move you out of a place of disaster and into a place of gains. Ideally, you want to transform your obstacles into an opportunity. In all situations, there is going to be an opportunity.

7. Donate

Make sure that you are giving of your energy, time, and financial resources when you can afford to be. Join a cause that is dear to you because you are grateful for what you have been able to earn. Donating allows you to live in gratitude because you help people and causes that you care about, and those who are less fortunate.

Know in your heart that the Universe is good, and while life can and will be hard at times, our attitude plays a big role in the way we experience things.

CHAPTER 7

BELIEVING YOU CAN

Of all of the negative emotions out there that can hurt your chances of attracting the things you desire, fear is the strongest one. Have you ever felt frightened, stressed, and anxious when you think about how your life is turning out? If you have, then you're in good company. However, it's important that you come up with a strategy for changing those thought patterns. Fear will hold you back and will make sure that you remain focused on those thoughts of lack, but love will fill you with positivity and will improve your energy vibrations so that you are able to manifest things. We are going to take a moment to look at some ways to work out those fears so that you can turn them into love and believe in the process.

To Radiate Love

If you have the admirable goal of transforming the universe with love, you must first learn how to transform yourself and your relationships. This can be done by raising your consciousness to match the vibration of love and radiate that as often as you can.

Humans can radiate love if they open their hearts to their self, others, and life.

Energetically, light travels through space, is pulled into a gravity field, and then attracts matter. This attraction turns into through, which talks to our body, and then the information, which helps to guide us to act, think, feel, or speak, and is our connection to our soul. When channeled through the heart, light energy changes into a human's capability of manifesting intentions to create a reality. People who love will be able to send out vibrations at a high frequency, but a person who finds it hard to love will emit at a lower frequency. The law of love suggests that the energy we share out will attract more of that same energy.

Let's look at it from the point of view of manifesting a healthy and loving relationship. Of course, relationships aren't the only reason to send out love, it is the easiest one to see.

Let's say that when you grew up you experienced some traumatic experiences in your life in relation to the idea of love. It could be that you were cheated on, sexually abused, or got your heart broken. Of course, while like attracts like, not everything that happens to you is your fault. There are times, such as assault of any kind, where you are simply the unfortunate victim for no fault of your own. The fault lies within the other person.

If you did experience anything traumatic like this, whenever you think back on those moments, you will likely experience a lot of painful emotions. You may even physical start shaking, crying, or experiencing the pain all over again.

Because of these past "love" experiences, when you try to approach a loving relationship, you are probably going to have a guard up. You have previously been hurt, so you want to make sure that you are protected from getting hurt again. This causes you to be closed off. You are afraid to be open because that means you are vulnerable. This causes you to resistant to letting another person.

This issue is rooted in fear. You are now afraid of being hurt, so you feel the need to protect yourself. Fear causes you to close yourself off, retreat, and prevents you from taking any sort of action. It will cause you to repel love. Since you live in this state of fear, you aren't allowing in love in. The only way to bring love into your life is to let go of those past fears and the emotions connected to them. The longer you hold onto all of that pain, the more you are going to repel love.

When you are able to emanate love, you ascend to your highest level of soul potential. This means that you end up performing better at world, are healthier, more creative, and impact the environment in a positive way. This is the time to realize that you are a change agent of love. To change the planet, you have to elevate your vibration and plant seeds of love throughout the environment.

If more people harnessed the energy of love and changed their negative emotions and thoughts to positive ones, we would create the strongest transformational power the world has ever seen. When we are able to shit to positive emotions and thoughts, our hearts naturally radiates a harmonic electromagnetic energy field that is able to positively affect the environment and every living being.

When you work to change your actions, thoughts, and word, you are able to change your life and the whole world. When you have this type of knowledge, you can see yourself as a powerful source of energy and get rid of self-defeating roles that you may have taken on, like being greedy and needy, dominating others, or playing the powerless victim. You are able to listen to yourself and no longer follow the ideas, direction, or belief systems of others.

Releasing Your Fears

If you want to find that place of love, you first have to learn how to work through your fear. This is going to require you to analyze your worries and to find what is causing your unhappiness. This is a lot easier said than done, and it can end up getting scary for some people.

Most like to ignore the fears they have because they are afraid of what they might find if they looked into them. If you want to become emotionally strong and manifest the things you want, you are going to have to face those problems instead of hiding from them.

1. Embrace and Master

It is very important to understand that transforming fear into love doesn't have to do with denying or repressing how your truly feel. Being able to master your emotions is a very useful skill. The idea is that you are able to fully embrace those emotions, acknowledge them, and then find a way to process them so that you can release them. Some great ways to do this is to write in a journal, release them through creativity like playing music or painting, or channel them into physical activities, like boxing, dancing, horse riding, and running.

2. Write Fears Down

While this might seem a bit counterintuitive, since you will be forced to focus on your fears, facing your problems head on is important in letting the go. You have to find the courage to sit down and write out the things that have been bugging you. Doing this can help to show you that some of your fears are likely ridiculous once they are put on paper. This makes it easier to forget about them.

On the other hand, you may end up discovering some fears that you didn't even know you had. Don't worry, though, this is a good things. Most of us have fears that are bugging us, but we have worked to hide them for so long that we subconsciously hid them and we don't realize they are still there. Finding those hidden fears is a good thing because once you have brought them to the surface, you can being to process them.

3. Demystify Fears

Most of the power that fear has is the fact that they aren't they well understood. For example, think about those times when you have felt this crawling unease, a pounding hear, or fear of failure without fully understand what is scaring you or why. In order to create more space for love and to reduce the power of fear, deliberately try to understand fear. Face it head on and start to figure out where its roots are, what it is representing, how it relates to how you view yourself. In most cases, you will start to find your limiting beliefs which have been holding you back. Then you can start to use affirmations and a focus wheel in order to replace those beliefs for new, positive ones.

Replacing Your Fears

Once you have taken the time to face your fears, and they are no longer a secret, you can then start to get rid of them. You have made the most important first step already. You have become conscious about your condition, and you have given yourself the power to change your relationship to fear. Let's look at some ways to help you interact with fear in a completely different way.

1. Do Good

At the end of the day, all we all want is to be heard, truly seen by others, and valued. Consequently, the most powerful gesture you could make is to sit down with another person and provide them with a non-judgmental ear to whatever they would like to say. Provide them with empathy, be fully present, and work to understand them. This type of love helps to make a world of difference to that other person, and it will feel you with compassion. Then, when you start to feel fearful, think about how you could offer love this way, and then change your attention to doing that.

2. Connect A Special Object to Your Transformation

You may have a specific object that you have connected to your law of attraction goal, so why not do the same for turning fear into love? You could find a small rock to do this with because you can hold it easily in your hand. When you do, imagine fear pouring into that rock and then love being sent out of the rock and soaking through your skin. Another idea would be to include a piece of jewelry that you could wear all the time as a simple reminder to focus on love. You can also choose a candle that has a scent that helps you to feel peaceful.

3. Stay Open

It is very natural to shut down when you are experiencing fear, even if you tend to be an open person. Whenever you start to feel fear undermining you, fight to keep your heart and mind open to all possible routes. Start to ask yourself what you could do in order to feel better in the situation you are in, take tiny but sure steps out of that comfort zone, and allow others to care for you when they say they want. Don't hide all of your worries, or yourself, away. Use the support system you have created, and know that there is absolutely no shame in being vulnerable.

4. Share Love

One way to share love is to show understanding and compassion to people around you. However, there are other ways to do this. For example, you can practice meditations that involves heart imagery of sending love out to others. Whether you make this a community in need, a person who is a bad place, or simply someone that you want to wish them the best. This little act can help to bring you in tune with abundance, placing you in the best place possible to manifest what you are looking to get. Plus, you can also follow the idea of doing a random act of kindness each day.

Doubting The Law of Attraction

This is the most common area where people will begin to experience fear and doubt. They worry about whether or not the law of attraction is actually working for them. This creates resistance. This is normal, and can be a good thing because it lets you know about any limiting beliefs or resistance that you may have. Once you know that these exist within you, you can start to get rid of them so that they are no longer holding you back.

There's a good chance that if you work through all of the steps above, it is going to get rid of some of that anxiety your have been feeling and you will start to believe that you are on the right track. That said, there are things you can do to work through fears that are connected to manifesting. The first thing you need to do is to bring yourself out of this world of fear. You don't have to worry about whether or not the law of attraction is working. You have to trust and believe that it is working and is unfolding as it should.

Understanding that you have the potential to change. If you experience fear or worry, then you likely have an unresolved problem. But, this problem can be changed. You can choose to change it. The important thing is to make sure you are willing to change.

Once you take the time to find out where you fear is actually coming from, then you can start to get rid of them. Eventually, you will come to a point where you realize things have shifted. You don't feel worried or scared. You start feel at peace and any worries that may come up, you are able to face from a neutral place.

Don't fall into the trap of not recognizing love simply because it doesn't look how you think it should. Remember what Oprah said, "When love doesn't come wrapped in our personal fantasy, we fail to recognize it."

CHAPTER 8

VISUALIZATION

Visualization is a skill that is often used in manifesting work and allows you to picture the things that you want in life. The better you can visualize your goals, the better the manifestation process is going to work. When you visualize, you are tricking the mind into thinking things are real. The emotions and feelings that you think up while visualizing are so close to reality that the mind believes they are real.

If you can picture yourself sitting on a tropical island, sipping a drink out of coconut, the water lapping at your feet, the sun on your skin, and the squishing sand under your toes, it can change how you feel. How does this make you feel? Our minds are so powerful that just that moment in time, while you are visualizing, you get completely transported there and you can actually feel these emotions and things.

Visualization is important since it bridges the gap between reality and fantasy. Sitting on a beach isn't a fantasy. It is actually more real than you realize. It isn't something that is out of reach. When you can learn to visualize regularly, nothing will be out of your reach. It could become a new normalcy for you. You can see yourself as an athlete, a sportsman, a rock star, or a writer.

The things you dream about you can create. Whatever the mind conceives, the mind will be able to achieve. Using visualization daily can help the law of attraction work better for you. It can help you make an image in your head about everything that you want in life. It also tells the Universe everything you want to attract in your life. If you want a promotion, visualize moving into a new office that has your name on the door and getting a large check. Visualization can help you find your goals, focus on them, and then manifest them. This in turn will help you create a motivated, positive mindset.

The Power of Visualization

When you take the time to visualize, you have to create images that could be physical or mental that depicts your future and goals in strong positive messages. There are many different tools you can use to help you accomplish this.

There have been several studies that have shown this is strong body and mind connection, and visualization works because the brain doesn't see the difference between your thoughts about action and actually taking action. To be successful when you visualize your goals, you have to make more of an effort to practice and develop your visualization. You can't simply sit around and fantasize about your perfect life or anything else you want to manifest. It is better to start visualizing small things that you need in your daily life than trying to start out with huge dreams and wind up getting disappointed.

Why Visualization is Important

When you visualize, it can help you create your dream life and there are techniques that have been used by successful people to reach their goals. There are several reasons why visualization is important and it gives you benefits, too:

- Visualization helps relieve stress: When you visualize, you are in a calm state of mind. This helps to clear your mind while getting rid of any stress and worry that you might have.

- Helps you have more confident: The more you can visualize you reaching your dreams and goals, the more confident you will begin to feel.
- Helps program your brain: When you visualize, it can help program the brain to recognize and find ways to manifest your goals and dreams. This makes it easier for you to begin using the law of attraction.
- Helps strengthen motivation: visualization can help you feel more excited and motivated that in turns helps you create the life you want.

Techniques for Visualization

There are some effective but easy techniques that you can use to improve your visualization skills:

- Magic Check

A great visualization tool is called a Magic Check. You can use this to attract financial freedom or wealth and so much more. The idea behind this it to write out a check to yourself in the amount that you would like to see in your bank account. It might also be a goal to land a new job or to find your perfect mate.

A magic check needs to be put somewhere that you can see all day, every day. This might be next to your bed so you see it when you wake up and when you go to bed. You can keep it in your wallet or purse. This magic check doesn't have to be just about finances. Whatever goal you have in mind, just write it on the check and be sure you feel good about the things you would like to manifest.

Give your check fuel with all the positivity you can give it. Always pretend that you have this amount of money already or the goal that you would like to achieve.

- Meditation

This is a great tool that helps you learn to visualize when you are visualizing at a time when your mind is present and clear. Once you learn how to meditate, you begin to get more access to your inner thoughts and feelings than you ever did before. Since you are always fully in the moment, you can really focus on your aspirations, goals, and yourself. While you are meditating, you need to send out positive energy, create a positive space, and visualize your goals.

Meditating can help your brain release all negative energy. It gives you brain enough space to travel wherever it needs to go. This is why visualization is extremely helpful. You will be able to have very strong visualization when you meditate since you are allowing your brain to do it for you, while you are getting rid of all negative energy.

- Daily Affirmations

We have talked about affirmation in this book already but these are such simple tools that can help your reshape your beliefs and help you move toward your goals. Affirmations have to be spoken and repeated daily. You could also do visual affirmations if you want to.

One way to do your affirmations is to stand in front of a mirror and say: "I love having a great job and being happy with myself." You can use this affirmation if you want to find a better job and if you have low self esteem. You goal might be feeling happy with yourself.

The law of attraction works with your energies and thoughts as they are recognized by the Universe. This is how you can put energy and positive affirmations into the world and get the Universe to respond to it. Repeating affirmations plays a huge role in the law of attraction. The more we can tell ourselves something, the more the message gets accepted by our subconscious and this in turn gets manifested.

- Dream Boards

These are also called vision boards. They are a way you can visually show your dreams, whether they are spiritual, romantic, or financial. Making a dream board is very inexpensive and an extremely creative way to connect with your goals for your future. Your dream board could be made by using whatever you have available, whether it is pictures from magazines, drawings, or things in nature.

When you are creating your vision board, you will showing you dreams and visions in physical ways along with reinforcing your affirmations. Your dream board needs to be unique and personal for you. Whatever you find that inspires and motivates you needs to be put on the board. You should hang your vision board in your bedroom or in your office. You will have it there to keep you motivated and in your mind.

Creative Visualization

Creative visualization is a great tool that helps you manifest your goals and helps attract the things you want in your life. Creative visualizations can help you get a better understanding about what you want out of life and to create the life you've always wanted. Let's talk about what creative visualization is and the way it works.

What is Creative Visualizations?

This is a kind of mindfulness exercise that could be used to bring you success in every area of your life. This is the process of putting together visual images about the things you want to bring into your life. You will begin to feel emotions that are associated with these images. Basically, creative visualization is where you imagine the things you want and then experience the feeling or emotions you would have if you actually had them.

This helps you put your desires and goals into the Universe and you will begin feeling motivated to reach them. This is similar to dream or vision boards that we talked about earlier but the images are in your mind.

Creative Visualization could be very powerful because you are using your mind's eye to make extremely detailed pictures about what you would like to manifest. This helps you feel more motivated and positive to reach your goals. After you have visualized, you will feel inspired and you will be ready to take actions to reach your goals.

Get as creative as you can with your visualizations. Even if you aren't a very creative person, it might surprise you to find how great it feels when you make something that shows your dreams. This can be done by making graphics on the computer, writing, drawing, or painting. Some find this way of visualization better because they have a better outlet for the dreams and goals. You can hang this anywhere you can see it. Creating your own art makes it more unique and personal for you.

The Power of the Mind

If you are always repeating specific thoughts to yourself, your mind automatically accepts these thoughts and this can cause a change to your mindset. When you change your mindset, it can change your habits, feelings, and behaviors. This is why creative visualizations are so effective.

The mind is powerful and the images it can create can determine some strong emotions and feelings that you might experience when you think about them. This is why you have to be completely clear about the things you want to visualize and the reasons behind them.

Creative visualization can help you manifest and achieve the outcomes that you want. These thoughts will be repeated constantly through your mind which can change your mindset and your behavior, in ways that will manifest your goals.

Creative visualization could be used as a therapeutic application. This is when visual imagery is used to recreate and replace things that cause you stress or upset you. This is done with a therapist, or as a part of a group. Creative visualization can help increase mental and physical relaxation while decreasing stress.

Benefits of Creative Visualization

Now that you know about the basics of visualization, let's look at the benefits. Here are six benefits that you can get from creative visualization:

- Improved Relationships

Creative visualization can help you improve your relationships. This could be either your partner or friends. While you visualize you getting more confident in your abilities and yourself, it can improve your relationships and social life while your overall well being is being improved.

- Gives Inspiration

Visualizations could give you a huge dose of inspiration, too. Once you visualize your dreams and goals, you will become inspired to make sure they come true. This inspiration could spur you to take the needed action toward your goals.

When you can see your goals in a visualization it will inspire you to make sure you see it in your reality, too.

- Brings Joy

Although your visualization might not be true at this very moment, just thinking about it will bring joy into your life. This happens because your mind isn't going to know the difference between the actual thing and the visualization.

This basically means that you will experience excitement and joy that you would feel as if it were actually real, this only makes your visualizations stronger.

- Self Confidence

When you use creative visualizations, you are picturing yourself experiencing positive situations and reaching success. This means your self confidence will increase since you will be beginning to believe in yourself and this will help your visualization come true faster.

The more you can visualize yourself doing these amazing things, the more confident you will become.

- Increase Focus

Similar to meditation, you can increase your concentration and focus by just sitting down and visualizing. Once you do some creative visualization, you will forgetting about your troubles and any worries that you may have about your future. This allows you to just concentrate and focus on your visualization.

- Reduce Stress

When you take the time to just sit still, be silent, and relax while visualizing, it can help you feel more positive about yourself and lessens your stress. Visualization is a type of relaxation that is similar to meditation. Since you will be visualizing positive situations, it can help you quiet your mind and help you feel relaxed.

CHAPTER 9

TRUSTING THE PATH

Another important aspect about manifesting money and other things is trusting the path that you are on. This plays into believing that the law of attraction is working for you. If you can't fully trust and faith and determination in what you are doing and the path you are on, you are going to struggle to get what you want.

Faith

Have you ever asked the Universe for anything but nothing ever happened? Have you been praying every day but nothing has changed?

The key to the Universe answering your prayers is having faith. Faith is all about letting go of those prayers. You have to tell yourself: "Whatever is meant to be will be. The Universe knows best. If I am meant to have it, I will have it. If not, then that is okay. All is well."

Yes, it can be hard to live on faith alone. Why do we ask the Universe for things if we were okay not ever getting them? Well, first of all, faith isn't about giving up. You aren't exactly giving up on the Universe or your dreams.

Rather, you are acknowledging that everything is fine and it will continue that way because the Universe knows what you need. Faith is about knowing there aren't just two things that you need to do in order to get the Universe's help: ask and then receive.

At times there might be factors that are involved in the Universe answering your prayers that you won't be aware of when you pray. These factors could keep you from getting your prayers answered.

Look at this example: You have asked the Universe for help finding a job. You have also asked for a good employer who treats their employees well and pays you a good salary. You would like to have a job that is permanent. You want a job that lets you use your skills. All these elements need to be created. Even if you want to have a job right now, it is going to take some time for the Universe to make things come together exactly the way you want them.

You have to also remember that each time you have doubts about whether or not the Universe is listening, or you begin to feel impatient or anxious, you are letting the Universe know that you don't enough faith that your prayers are going to be answered.

If you want the Universe to answer prayers, you have to have faith that the Universe will provide.

Determination

When working with the law of attraction, taking action is critical when trying to manifest things. If you just sit around saying positive affirmation after positive affirmation and just waiting on things to appear magically, you are going to be waiting for a long, long time. But if you begin taking action but you don't have the right energy behind it, you might manifest the complete opposite of what you want. If you have an energy of determination, this is a very different energy than energy of desperation. If you begin thinking about determination, you might bring up feelings of strength, steadiness, and persistence. If you begin to think about desperation, you might begin feeling scattered, stressed, and anxious. When you have determination, you will build momentum. When you feel desperate, you might see some short-term success that isn't sustainable and becomes nothing but chaos.

How could you make sure that you are beginning at the right place?

To be able to manifest the things you want successfully, it is going to take the right alignment. You have to have an alignment of your actions, emotions, and thoughts. And more than anything else, you have to dream. The following order works the best for me.

- Dreams

Let's start with your dreams. You have to be absolutely sure about the things you want to manifest. You need to get super picky here. The more details you can give to it, the better. You have to be absolutely sure on every quality of your dream like what will it taste like, smell like, sound like, and look like. How are you going to feel once you are living your dream? These details are extremely important. Don't fret about the details on when, where, how, or who. These details will slow you down or stop you since they will dictate how you would like for your manifestation to be delivered. This isn't up to you. That is for the universe to determine.

- Thoughts

After you are perfectly clear on everything you want, now is the time to get in alignment with these things. Begin with thoughts. You have to focus on the things you want just like you already have them. You need to say affirmations that begin with the words "I AM" are the strongest because they are telling the universe that you are claiming your dreams. Make sure you say them in a positive way. You would say: "I am financially abundant" rather than saying "I am debt free." The last one brings you a mentality that is lacking.

- Energy

Once you have your thoughts taken care of now you need to work on your energy. Go back to the way you want to feel once you are living your dreams. You have to get in that place right this very moment. Practice feeling those feelings. You have the ability to call up that type of energy. This is a critical step since the wrong energy is going to bring you the wrong results. The easiest way for you to raise your energy is practicing gratitude. Think about all the abundance you have already and you are going to be attracted to even more.

So do you have your thoughts in place? What about your emotions and energy? If you have all of this, it is time to take action. Don't worry about it if you don't have a complete strategy in place, if you just begin, the path will unfold in front of you. After you take that first step from your inspiration into determination, you will enjoy everything that this energy is going to magnify. Your determination is going to take over and your momentum is going to build.

Success Stories

It's easy to say that you have to trust the path and believe that it is all going to work out, but it's another to really believe those things. To help you out, let's take a look at a couple of celebrity success stories. While we like to believe that celebrities are these lucky people who got their success thrust upon them, most of them had to work hard to get where they are. They didn't get their because of luck. They set goals, they talked to the universe, and they took action steps to get to where they wanted.

Jim Carey

The video of Jim Carrey talking about how he used the law of attraction has made the rounds on social media sites many times over. But encase you haven't heard. I'll tell you what he did.

Before he made it as a big movie star, back in the late '80s, he used to go to Mulholland Drive every night and picture himself having directors interested in him and people telling him that they like his work. He would visualize the things he wanted coming into his life. During this time, he had nothing. His visualization was something he did to make him feel better. He would tell himself that he did have those things; he just didn't have a hold of them yet.

Guess where he got this idea? From the self-help section of the bookstore. He also took things a step beyond visualizations. He wrote himself a check. He sat down and wrote himself a check for ten million dollars for acting services rendered. He set himself a goal of five years to reach this goal. He dated the check Thanksgiving 1995. He stuck the check in his wallet and kept it there.

And just before Thanksgiving 1995, he found out that he got the part in *Dumb and Dumber*, where he made ten million dollars. But, to round things out, he explained that visualization works if you work hard. That's a theme you are going to see here. While law of attraction will bring you what you want, you have to show the Universe that you are willing to work for it.

Steve Harvey

Steve Harvey is an actor, talk show host, and game show host. On his talk show, he has spoken about the book *The Secret*. This book was really the book that shot the law of attraction into the mainstream, and this book just happens to be a self-help book that resonates with Steve Harvey.

Like attracts like is the first concept that Steve talks about. He explains that what you are is what you will get. If you are negative, you get negativity, but if you're positive, you get positivity. He also explains how what you can picture in your mind, you can hold in your hand.

Then he goes on to talk about ask, believe, receive. He talks about how people will freeze up because they don't know how to get somewhere or get something. But you don't have to know-how. All you have to do is ask, believe that it will happen, and you will get it. He then moves on to explain gratitude. He says in order to make it to the next level, you must be grateful for where you are in this moment.

He wraps things up with "laughter attracts joy and release negativity." Laughter brings joy into your life and makes you happier. He explained how he was a mess the week after his mama died. The minister said that they should think about the good things that she had done, and then he and his brothers started thinking about this and smiling. He then said the minister said one more thing, "joy and depression cannot reside in the same place." He said that you need to laugh at everything, even if it isn't funny, "just laugh."

Oprah Winfrey

Jim Carey shared his visualization story on the Oprah Winfrey Show, so what better person to move onto than Oprah herself. She is a philanthropist, producer, actress, and talk show host. She has been a long-time advocate for the law of attraction because of the way it changed her life. In one interview with Larry King, she explained how the law of attraction helped her get a role in the movie, *The Color Purple.*

She did the movie in 1985, but she had read the book prior to that. When she read the book, she went out and got copies for everybody she knew because she was obsessed with the book. She moved to Chicago and then get a call from a casting director asking if she wanted to audition for a role. She had never gotten a call from anybody for anything like this at this point in her life. Her was response was, "Is this *The Color Purple?*" The casting director said, "No, it's for *Moonsong.*" She explains that she had been praying for *The Color Purple.*

She goes to the audition and it was for the movie *The Color Purple.* She auditions and doesn't hear anything back for a while. She gets depressed about this and goes to a "fat farm" because she thinks she didn't get the part because she was too fat. While at this fat farm, she is trying to let this go. She is upset that she hasn't heard anything back and has been utterly obsessed with the thoughts of getting cast in the movie. Then a woman comes out and tells her that she has a phone call.

The call was from Steven Spielberg asking her to come in. She didn't know Steven Spielberg or Quincy Jones before all of this. All she knew was that she wanted to be a part of *The Color Purple.* Quincy Jones happened to see her on AM Chicago and knew that she was meant to be Sophia.

CHAPTER 10

WHAT TO DO ONCE YOUR MONEY REACHES YOU

Within the financial world the word "appreciation" has two components. In a quantitative realm, appreciation is the increasing value of your financial assets. In a qualitative realm, appreciation is feeling grateful for your circumstances and financial resources.

Both of these elements are very important, but it is the qualitative mindset that is best to increase our well-being and wealth in life. Lynne Twist says that thinking appreciatively is the complete opposite of thinking scarcity. She says: "When your attention in on all the things that are scarce and lacking, in your town, family, work, or life, then it becomes what you are about."

Jackie Kems thinks that we need to pay more attention to growth. She states: "Our attention will create our experience, and if we focus on lack, we create more lack."

Due to all the past programming we've had, many of us have created habits of just focusing on all the things that go wrong with our finances instead of all the things that are going well. We have a tendency to find all the problems that have to be fixed instead of noticing all the things that have been going well.

The truth of the matter is, when we pay attention to the breakdowns and problems with money, and then this is where consciousness will live. If there isn't a counterbalance to this, we will continue thinking about our obstacles and limitations instead of all the possibilities and abundance.

This is why it is best to look at all the positive aspects in life while focusing on all the values that we have to create more. This is why we need to appreciate all the things we have because "what we appreciate appreciates." Everything you focus on will grow larger.

You can use simple visualization exercises that will help nurture this positivity. It begins by reflecting on certain areas in your life like learning, work, finances, community, and family. Then you will make a list of all the things that are most important to them in all of these domains, and then imagine what they want to achieve or experience in your future. These questions can help guide your thinking:

1. What things to you value most in every area of your life?
2. What are the "riches" in every area of your life?
3. Which "riches" do you want to have in every area of your life in your future?

This exercise can help you appreciate all the things you already have, but it can help you imagine your versions of a meaningful, rich life in the future. The clearer this visualization is, the more it will guide your choices you make and will help shape your life that you want to have.

Do you realize that you already have abundance? It doesn't matter who you are, where you were raised, or what your situation is, you have always been abundant. This happens because you were born in a universe where all types of resources are plentiful.

How can we learn to notice and then appreciate your abundance to be able to attract a lot more? If you can follow these tips to increase your success and find out how to appreciate all that you have and find happiness with yourself. Plus, you will learn that you have all the tools that you need to live your dream life.

How to Find Happiness

- Get Into Nature

Ask yourself the questions:

1. Has anyone figured out a way to end the universe that we live in?
2. Is there a quota on the amount of air that we need in order to survive?
3. Are there any limits on the sun's ability to give us heat, light, or energy?

If you look at nature, you are going to find all kinds of sources that show us we live in a world that has unlimited amounts of energy, and this means unlimited abundance.

Everything in life is energy. Money is energy. Happiness is energy. Love is energy. If there are any restrictions on how much of these things that we are capable of experiencing are the ones we put on ourselves.

- Focus on The Happiness Inside

This universe is so abundant that it brings us whatever we choose to focus on. If you focus on abundance, you will attract more abundance. If you only focus on what you don't have, you will only experience more of what you don't have.

Think about all the seven billion people who are living on this planet just like you. While you are thinking about all these people of various backgrounds, value systems, and ages who are living their lives on Earth, how many versions of "reality" do you think are being experienced with these people? Their experiences fall in a very drastic continuum. Some get surrounded by all kinds of abundance while other people are struggling but never have enough.

How do you account for these drastic variations in your life experiences?

Yes, all the conditions that we find ourselves in have to do with how happy or miserable we feel daily. But the one question that nobody has asked yet is: "how do those conditions come into our experience in the first place?"

Abundance is one of countless life experiences that is possible for all of us if we can realize that it will unfold when you are willing to direct our attention to finding the evidence that it exists.

- Change Your Thought Patterns

The things you see when you look at your life circumstances isn't reality. It is just the way you perceive that reality gets filtered through your beliefs. There are some beliefs that can put you in alignment with all the abundance that you want while other will keep you from achieving it.

If you think that resources are scarce and in order to have wealth means you have to sacrifice things in your personal life, or the hardships from your past keep holding you back from creating happiness, they will get rid of the abundance that is your birthright.

It would be like we are standing on the edge of a river that is rushing and swollen with sweet, fresh water but all you have to carry water in is a thimble. Just like this river, abundance can travel on the path of least resistance. Water can't get through any area where there is opposing beliefs so it just runs its course and goes around all the rocks.

When you can learn to shift your beliefs and affirm that there is plenty of everything to go around, you will realize that you are valuable and deserve everything that can come your way. It is possible to have abundant amounts of money doing the things you love. You will make that space inside of larger so that you can receive more.

Appreciating everything that you are experiencing right now is the key to help shift your beliefs about your future.

- Celebrate Your Life Right Now

Look at your life and how it exists right now. You will probably find some realities that you are living with that were at one time just a daily goal.

It might be the house that you are in, the relationship you are in, your friends, or your career was at one time something that only existed as a dream or idea. Keep in mind that there are many aspects of your life and yourself that are going very well! Many of these things sustain themselves with no effort from you. You just have to find the happiness that lives inside you.

Remember that you have all the air you need to breathe, you have food to eat, and water to drink… these are all good reasons to celebrate. Knowing you live in harmony with nature and all her beauty… this is a reason to celebrate. Knowing you were born with your five senses that allow you to experience these things daily is a big reason to celebrate.

You are a unique person, and you are on this Earth for your own unique purpose. You are very interested in your own self-discovery and this is one more reason for a celebration.

Appreciation's energy is the most attractive in the entire universe. Any time you get appreciated by other people, you feel inspired, validated, safe, and seen. This inspires you to do even more. When you appreciate other things or other people, you will generate the same level of emotions inside yourself. This is due to the fact that you can't appreciate your surroundings without bathing in its energy.

As the 17th century French historian and writer, Voltaire stated:

"Appreciation is a wonderful thing: It makes what is excellent in others belong to us as well."

When you can improve your relationship with money, you will be able to create financial abundance in your life.

CHAPTER 11

HONORING YOUR VALUE

You have probably heard several words that begin with self such as self-care, self-love, self-confidence, self-respect, self-acceptance, self-compassion, self-esteem, and so on.

There are numerous words that can help us describe the way we feel about ourselves, the way we think of ourselves, and the way we act toward ourselves. It is completely normal that these begin blending together, but they are various concepts all with their own unique purposes, findings, and meanings.

Keep reading to learn about all the most important "self" word and that is self-worth.

Is There A Difference Between Self-Value and Self-Worth?

Self-value and self-worth are two terms that are related and are sometimes used interchangeably. If you have a sense of self-worth, this means that you value yourself. If you have a sense of self-value it means that you believe you are worthy. The main difference between these two is small enough that both could be used to describe the same concept.

Some people look at self-value as being a "more behavioral than emotional, more about how you act toward what you value, including yourself, than how you feel about yourself compared to others."

Self-Esteem Versus Self-Worth

There isn't a big difference between these two either, especially for people who aren't professional psychologists. If you look on the Merriam-Webster website for the definition of self-worth, you are going to see the very first definition is "self-esteem."

You will find similar definitions on the various dictionary websites out there. Most of these terms are used to describe the same concepts or ideas but for people who are immersed in these, there is a difference. Dr. Hibbert explains it the best:

"Self-esteem is what we think and feel and believe about ourselves. Self-worth is recognizing that you are greater than all of those things. It is a deep knowing that you are of value, that you are loveable, you are necessary in this life, and you are of incomprehensible worth."

Self-Confidence Versus Self-Worth

Along the same lines as above, there are some subtle but huge differences between self-confidence and self-worth.

Self-confidence isn't an evaluation of yourself. It is more about feeling cometent and having confidence in certain areas of life. You might have a good amount of self-worth but you don't have that much confidence when talking about specific school subjects, sports, or being able to speak a foreign language.

You don't have to have a lot of self-confidence in all areas of your life because there are going to be some things that you just won't be good at, and then there are going to be areas where you excel. The main thing is that you have self-confidence in all the activities that you do like to do and maintain a high self-worth at all times.

Psychology Behind Self-Worth

Within psychology, self-worth isn't a popular topic to research. It isn't as popular as self-confidence or self-esteem, but this isn't saying that it isn't as important. Self-worth is the very core of ourselves, our behaviors, feelings, and thoughts are ties to the way we see our value and worthiness as humans.

Theory Behind Self-Worth

This theory states that a person's priority in life should be to find self-acceptance and this is usually found by achieving things. And of course, achievements are normally found by competing with others.

Because of this, the logical conclusion would be that competing with other people could help you feel like you have made some impressive achievements and this will make you feel even more proud of yourself and will enhance the way you accept yourself.

This theory states that there are four elements to this model:

- Ability
- Effort
- Performance
- Self-Worth

The top three work with one another to help a person figure out their self-worth. Your effort and ability will have a large impact on your performance, and all of them can contribute to your feelings of value and worth.

Even though this theory shows that understanding self-worth as we experience it, it is not good that we put all our emphasis on the things that we achieve. Other than competing and "winning," there are other factors that could contribute to our self-worth.

What Can Help Determine Self-Worth?

Well, according to the theory, our self-worth gets determined by how we evaluate our performance in the activities that you think are valuable.

But people still use yardsticks to try and measure their self-wroth. Here are some factors that people have tried to use to compare and measure their self-worth to others:

1. Your career or what you do: We have a tendency to judge other people by the things they do. Stockbrokers are considered to be more valuable and successful than a teacher or janitor.

2. Your social circle or who you know: Some people are going to judge they value and other people's value by their social status and the influential and important people that they know.

3. The things you achieve: Some people will use their achievement to figure out their worth like having a successful business, high SAT scores, or getting accepted into the college of their dreams.

4. Net worth: This means a person's financial assets, material possessions, or income.

5. Appearance: This can be measured several different ways from the type of attention a person gets from others, their size, or the number that shows on a scale.

You need to fix your misperceptions and misunderstandings about self-worth. Rather than listing all the things that determine self-worth, you need to find the things that don't determine your self-worth. The following is a list of things that you DO NOT need to worry about when figuring out your self-worth:

1. Anyone or anything but you: This is the heart of the matter. You and you alone are the only person who gets to determine your self-worth. If you truly believe that you are valuable and worthy, you are. Even if you don't truly believe that you are valuable and worthy, well, I am here to tell you that you are!

2. The things you like: So what if your acquaintances and friends don't think you have good taste or are sophisticated, of if you like the finer things in life, your worth remains the same.

3. How much money you have: As long as you have enough money where you can physically survive, then you have the maximum amount of worth that you can get out of money.

4. Your relationship: It doesn't matter if you are alone, dating, or in a committed relationship.

Your value remains that same because your relationships don't change your worth.

5. How many friends you have: Your value doesn't have anything to do with the number of friends or people you know. The quality of these relationships is all that matters.

6. Your grades: Every single person in the world has their own weaknesses and strengths and some just don't do well in class. This doesn't have any bearing on their worth as a human. A student who struggles in class is just as important as that straight A student.

7. How far can you run: This has to be the least important factor when determining your self-worth. If you like running and you feel better if you can improve your time, then great! If not, great! Being able to run a one-minute mile isn't going to determine your self-worth.

8. Other people: As stated before, it does not matter what people think about you or what they have accomplished or done in their life. Your fulfillment and satisfaction are more important that what other people are doing, saying, or thinking.

9. How old you are: You are never too old or too young for anything. How old you are is just a number and doesn't mean anything toward your value.

10. Your social media standings: It doesn't matter how many people follow you or you follow. It can be healthy and enlightening to look at other people's perspectives but their opinions don't have any impact on your value.

11. Your job: It does not matter what you do in life. The only thing that matters is that you do it well and you enjoy doing it.

12. Your to-do list: Reaching your goals is wonderful and it makes you feel good to get to cross things off of your list but it does not have any bearing on your worth.

Now that you know what self-worth is and isn't let's get to the root of what help establish our self worth. Let's start with my story:

I have spent most of my life hating myself. When I say I hated myself, I mean I hated every single thing about myself. I hated my straight hair because everybody else in my family had some curl to their hair. I hated my shortness because everyone else in my family was taller than me even my younger sister. There were times when I wished I were adopted so I could go find my real parents. But as an adult I looked back at my childhood and finally realized what had happened to make me feel this way.

I had a very critical mother who actually thought she was helping me when she was just tearing me down over and over again. She criticized everything about me. All those things that I hated about myself, she made sure to remind me of them all the time. She didn't just do this behind closed doors so to speak. It seemed like she would do her best to tell others just how "different" I was from the rest of the family.

I was very sensitive about my looks and her criticisms and attacks affected me more than she ever knew. Even though she didn't realize what she was doing, I took her hurtful words and attacks to heart and they ended up hurting my self-worth and psyche.

If a person in my life who was supposed to love me no matter what constantly said bad things about me, these things had to be true, right?

No, in fact, they were completely wrong.

While growing up, I went through many life events that were very rocky. I finally decided to confront my past and look at the things that had caused me to hate myself and my low self-worth.

I needed to deal with my childhood and all those things that I had pushed deep down inside me. You might have experienced some things that were similar to my experiences during childhood. Have you ever had moments when you just couldn't stand yourself?

Yes, I do mean actually loathing yourself or hating yourself. If you have ever felt like you just didn't belong in your own skin or you didn't want to be you anymore.

If your childhood was an environment that damaged you, where actions and words of other people actually hurt you and it went straight to your core. Let's look at some things you can do to help you feel more comfortable with yourself.

Give Your Fears and Doubts Some Kindness

All those voices in the back of your mind are just remnants of the people's voices in your life who have criticized you. You have grown up hearing harmful and disapproving language and words from the people who are supposed to love you.

You have heard all your life that you aren't worthy or good enough. You aren't talented, loving, skinny, or smart enough. These voices when mixed with your own inner voice can be very destructive. These voices will speak up anytime you begin doing anything in life.

Even before you get a chance to start, these voices will overwhelm you and sink you. You need to be more aware of these voices and move them out of the way. You can be polite and thank them for their concerns but tell them that you will be fine without them.

Take some time and ask yourself if these thoughts are coming from a place of fear or courage. The voices coming from doubts and fears should be pushed out of the way.

Embrace Your Feelings

Have you always run away from your feelings, hid them away, or tried to deny them? Have people told you that what you are feelings don't matter and you need to "get over it?" If you have suppressed your feelings, you will be in a constant state of denial and you won't feel connected to your true self.

There are some feeling that could be very distressing and painful but if you can learn to experience them, they will go away. The more you are able to feel your feelings, they won't have as tight of a control over you.

You have to be open to allowing your feelings to be there. You need to learn to sit with them and be one with them. You will be more comfortable with yourself once you aren't hiding your true feelings. Let all the feelings that you are experiencing to flow over you without any resistance. If they become too overwhelming, find someone you trust and talk about your feelings or you can write them in a journal. Sometimes, just getting them out will help you deal with them.

Embrace Your Failures and Mistakes

Do you beat yourself up about things you didn't do or did in your past? Do you let the past paralyze you so you can't enjoy your life? You have to realize that you aren't your failures or mistakes. You aren't all those experiences you had while growing up. You aren't all those hard relationships that you were in or all the hardships you've faced.

You have to realize that all those downs and ups in life have made you the person you are today. You don't have to feel ashamed or deny your pain. You need to completely embrace and accept everything that you have dealt with and confronted. By doing this, you will be able to live a powerful life.

Today, you are stronger because of all the failures and mistakes that you made in the past. Mistakes are just your experiences. Failures are just your wisdom. You need to embrace your story but don't let it define you.

Stop Comparing Yourself

People have compared you to others your whole life; your community, your coworkers, your teachers, and your family.

Reality shows, society in general, and social media has a big desire to rank people and this has caused you to believe that you aren't as good as others and other's will always be better.

You have to quit comparing yourself to others and using their standards as yours. Other people might be succeeding or doing work in the things that interest you, but you still don't feel adequate when you compare yourself to them.

Visualize your life as a race and the only person running in this race is you. Your life isn't about winning this race, it is about enjoying it. It is about living a meaningful and fulfilling life.

You have to begin living the life that you want rather than feeling inadequate anytime you compare yourself to others. Get rid of all those thoughts about being inadequate. Quit thinking that you aren't good enough or don't have enough to measure up to others. Anytime a comparison pops into your mind, tell yourself that having all those things that other people have isn't going to make you happy. You have to remain focused on your life.

Realize That You Are Enough

If people are constantly putting you down or comparing you to others, you probably think that you won't ever meet up to their expectations.

Everybody wants other people to embrace and validate them. They want bosses, significant others, family, and friends to tell them that they are enough and they are complete.

You soak up those messaged that tell you that you aren't enough spiritually, emotionally, financially, or physically. The big secret to achieving self-worth is just to realize that you have always been enough. You don't have to do anything more. You must need to be.

"Being" means you have to accept yourself just the way you are. It means understanding and self-awareness. It means you have compassion for yourself and you feel complete inside. It is realizing that you are complete right now. Nobody else's opinion about you matters.

You don't need to do anything else. There isn't one accomplishment or achievement that will make you enough.

You have to realize that you are enough and once you do, that is all you need.

You Have Principles… Live Them

You will be more in line with yourself if you can be honest with yourself. Everybody has a set of principles that guide them through life. It is sometimes hard to find these principles since your caregivers, society, and friends have influenced them heavily.

They have pressured you into doing some things that you didn't want to do and you are living a life that isn't yours. If you want to live in line with yourself, you have to live according to your own principles.

What principles run your life? Which values do you matter the most? Is it love, fairness, humor, equality, loyalty, fun, service, adventure, or family?

Look at your life and figure out all the things that you really care about. Write down all these values and figure out if your life embodies them. Do you live your life according to the things that matter to you or do you live another person's life?

In order to live your life, live it according to all the principles that matter the most to you.

Release Perfection and Expectations

If you were raised in a house that kept very high standards, you are going to always want to do more. You will set goals that aren't realistic and will always be looking for perfection.

This is what your caregivers wanted you to do, you won't ever be satisfied with the things you have. You will always strive for the highest levels of perfections. You won't ever be satisfied and you won't ever settle.

You have to acknowledge all these things and let them go. When you realize that you have been holding onto unhealthy expectations, you will be able to step away from your life and breathe easier.

When you are finally able to let go of all the unrealistic expectations and demands that you have, you will feel like a huge weight has been lifted from your shoulders.

Be Grateful for What You Have and Who You Are

If you grew up with criticism, you probably didn't take the time to be grateful. You were constantly dealing with verbal abuse, and your feelings of lack and inadequacy.

This is the time that you have to appreciate all the things you have in life and yourself. The best way to quit feeling unworthy or as if your life isn't perfect is to see all those things that you do have.

First and foremost... YOU. You have to be proud of all the things that you have done and who you are. If you are reading this right now, be happy that you have committed to improving yourself. If you are reading this on a tablet, be grateful for that tablet. If you area reading this on a computer, be grateful for your computer. If you have running water in your house, be grateful for that. If you have electricity, be grateful for that. If you have a car, be grateful for that. If you ate today, be grateful for that.

I think you can see where I am going with this. Learn to be grateful. Each morning when you wake up, try to write a list of ten things that you are grateful for. It might just amaze you that you will begin feeling more appreciative and love toward yourself.

It doesn't matter what happened to you during your life, just realize that you can change it.

Constantly caring for yourself and be the person that you know you are capable of being. Love and honor are the best gifts that you can give to yourself. You won't just be healing yourself but you will be sharing a new you with the world.

CONCLUSION

Thank you for making it through to the end of the book, let's hope it was informative and able to provide you with all of the tools you need to achieve your goals whatever they may be.

The next step is to start looking at the things you need to change about your mindset and how you have been thinking about money. Once you can spot the traps you have been falling into, you will be able to change them so that you no longer cause yourself more harm than good. This won't be an easy process, but it will be worthwhile once you start seeing your bank account increase. Remember, you can expect to earn a million dollars overnight. That's not realistic. Manifestation takes time, and happens at the right time. While you may feel right now is the best time, the Universe knows better. Trust in the process and know that things are happing even if you can't see them.

Finally, if you found this book useful in any way, a review on Amazon is always appreciated!

www.ingramcontent.com/pod-product-compliance
Lightning Source LLC
Chambersburg PA
CBHW071814080526
44589CB00012B/786